WHAT PEOPLE ARE SAYING ABOUT

POLIT]

Peter Mayo shows us ... original new book not only th... globalizing Mediterranean world (including the Arab world and its indignant youth), but he also provides us with most important insights about how to develop new concepts for the new learning situations. One common and most important element of Mayo's publication is that he underscores the political basis of education. He shows that education is not a neutral enterprise (unlike the way neoliberal economy presents it) but is serving either to 'domesticate' and strengthen the status quo of subaltern groups, or else 'liberate' in the sense of contributing to the ushering in of a new world in which principles of social justice and ecological sustainability are held uppermost. Education is viewed in the broadest sense, the way Gramsci viewed it, seeing it as central and integral to the workings of hegemony itself. This includes a more holistic view of critical engagement in the public sphere, 50 years after the release of Habermas' famous book on this issue.

Ursula Apitzsch, Professor of Political Science and Sociology, Goethe-University of Frankfurt/Main, whose many publications include, *Self Employment Activities of Women and Minorities. Their Success or Failure in relation to Social Citizenship Policies* (2008); *Care and Migration* (2010).

Peter Mayo's fascinating book is as timely as it is important. It is incisive and trenchant in its critique of global capitalism, and presents cogent and informative analyses of liberal and neoliberal policies that buttress it. It is courageous and provocative as it develops alternative perspectives on central social and political questions facing the world such as race, migration, education and socio-economic inequality. It is well written and well argued, as well as engaging and engaged. It is a book that will appeal to both the specialist and the general reader.

Benedetto Fontana, Political Science, Baruch College, CUNY, New York City, author of *Hegemony and Power: On the Relation Between Gramsci and Machiavelli* (1993), and co-editor of *Talking Democracy: Historical Perspectives on Rhetoric and Democracy* (2004).

Education and healthcare are spheres in which the failures of capitalism and neoliberalism are unmistakable and mounting. Peter Mayo's masterful book provides fabulous insight connecting Cuban successes in medicine and education, Nicaraguan literacy campaigns, the centrality of the crisis of higher education in Europe today and the recent uprisings in the Middle East. Working through particular cases of atrocity as well as success, Mayo gives an intimate sense of the obstacles and political possibilities facing us today. His broad conception of education and the continuing role of the state within global capitalism are essential. Emphasizing South-South cooperation and non-profit oriented exchange, Mayo provides hopeful alternatives to common North-South dynamics.

Peter Ives, Professor, Dept. of Politics, University of Winnipeg and author of *Gramsci's Politics of Language: Engaging the Bakhtin Circle and the Frankfurt School* (2004) and *Language and Hegemony in Gramsci* (2004).

Politics of Indignation is a challenging, accessible and exciting book. Not only does it provide a critical analysis of the neoliberal onslaught on public education across a range a countries, it also offers new insights into the dynamics of control, while demonstrating how and where resistance has succeeded. It is a hopeful book; it encourages and inspires the reader to act to protect public interest values in education, not least because action is shown to be effective in different contexts and countries. I strongly recommend it to all of those who wish to comprehend and to resist the attacks on public education.

Kathleen Lynch, UCD Equality Studies Centre, School of Social Justice, University College Dublin, Ireland – co-author of *New Managerialism in Education* (2012)

Politics of Indignation

Imperialism, Postcolonial
Disruptions and Social Change

Politics of Indignation

Imperialism, Postcolonial Disruptions and Social Change

Peter Mayo

Winchester, UK
Washington, USA

First published by Zero Books, 2012
Zero Books is an imprint of John Hunt Publishing Ltd., Laurel House, Station Approach,
Alresford, Hants, SO24 9JH, UK
office1@jhpbooks.net
www.johnhuntpublishing.com
www.zero-books.net

For distributor details and how to order please visit the 'Ordering' section on our website.

Text copyright: Peter Mayo 2012

ISBN: 978 1 78099 536 6

A CIP catalogue record for this book is available from the British Library.

Design: Stuart Davies

Printed and bound by CPI Group (UK) Ltd, Croydon, CR0 4YY

We operate a distinctive and ethical publishing philosophy in all
areas of our business, from our global network of authors to
production and worldwide distribution.

CONTENTS

Preface and Acknowledgments

We are living in hard though interesting times. They are hard times in the sense that ordinary people are being made to pay for the lavish greed of a few beneficiaries of the capitalist system, the 1 per cent, comprising CEOs and bankers, who have brought the world to almost inconceivable ruin, placing the burden of austerity squarely on the shoulders of the 99 per cent. They are also hard times because, in North Africa and the Middle East, legitimate human struggles for work, dignity and genuine democracy have been and are still being met with some of the most brutal repression. We witness the lengths that people are prepared to go to hang on to positions of autocratic power and privilege. These are hard times indeed, given that it is the prerogative of a small percentage of powerful people to determine who is allowed to thrive and whose life is dispensable; who is allowed to live and who is left to rot in abject conditions, as manifest in the wake of Hurricane Katrina or in situations when social expenditure, including expenditure on health, is cut as a result of austerity measures. These are hard, hard times as public spaces are constantly commodified and privatized; new commons are privately enclosed. Important aspects of social life such as health and education, as well as pensions, become a matter of individual instead of social responsibility. These are times when once greatly cherished public goods, such as education and health, become consumer products, none more so than higher education (HE) institutions where the quest for profits and lucrative international HE markets is given more importance than the quest for an education that contributes to the development of a democratic public sphere.

And yet we are also living in interesting times in which politics is rescued from the exclusive clutches of politicians and is constantly being played out in globalized public arenas such as the squares and streets of Athens, Madrid, Cairo, Tunis, New York and Damascus, as a clear groundswell of dissent, indignation and tenacity is manifest and beamed throughout all corners of the globe. This is the kind of stuff which makes one dream of 'another world' that 'is possible,' which lends credence to the cry reverberating through the various world and regional social forums. And yet the strong sense of hope fuelled by these events is necessarily tempered by caution and the fear of a 'false dawn' as caretaker regimes, following the deposition of an autocratic leader, drag their feet in ushering in much augured reforms. The threat of another civil war looms large in countries such as Libya, and certain autocratic regimes, as that in Syria, prove more resilient than others, backed by emerging economic and political powerhouses. The groundswell in the West lays bare the state's 'maximal,' as opposed to the much declared 'minimal,' presence as the repressive forces over which it holds a monopoly make their presence felt. Earlier this very same state put paid to the myth, exposed in Chapter 1 of this book, that its presence has been curtailed in neoliberal times. It intervened to bail out banks and provide rescue packages to help prop up a tottering economy. Meanwhile precarious living is the staple of everyday life for thousands of citizens, skilled or unskilled, formally well educated or otherwise, as much coveted well paid 'middle class,' career jobs are at a premium globally.

It is against these scenarios that, thanks to the encouragement of Henry Giroux, I have been engaged over the past year and a half in writing op ed and 'news analysis' columns for *Truthout* and *Counterpunch*, in addition to a number of other outlets, some international and others local (e.g. the Maltese branch of *Indymedia*). These writings enabled me to couch my ideas in a more popular and accessible idiom rather than in that style and register favored by the academic reviews in which I had been publishing most of my work throughout the past twenty years. These articles in *Truthout* and *Counterpunch* provide the basis for this book's chapters. The challenges included that of revising, updating and expanding some of the pieces and writing others, as I sought to construct an overarching thematic structure for this compendium.

The volume starts off with one of the themes just mentioned, namely the centrality of the state in an age governed by neoliberal policies. Neoliberalism constitutes one of the leitmotifs of this book. I therefore move on to discuss some of the origins of the neoliberal scenario with specific reference to what is commonly referred to, in Latin America, as the 'First September 11.' I do this to highlight the violence, symbolic and also physical, that marked the birth pangs of Neoliberalism which can sit comfortably not only with what is referred to as the 'new fascism' these days but also with fascism of the 'old school,' a coup d'état, such as that in Chile, leading to purges, executions and repression of the most horrific kind. Neoliberalism had its trial run in an orgy of bloodshed.

I then move on to explore an alternative revolutionary paradigm to the one ushered in through the first September 11, underlining the contradictions and strengths. The focus here is on the achievements of the Cuban and subsequently the Nicaraguan revolutions, also indicating the way the latter effort was eroded through time. The discussion on Cuba is co-authored with my Puerto Rican colleague and friend, Antonia Darder and owes its origin to our jointly penned preface, as series editors, to a text on Cuban education. I highlight, in the Nicaraguan case, the impact of external as well as internal forces. With respect to the latter, the theme of alliances or rather misplaced alliances is taken up with reference to the meaning of workers' solidarity in this day and age, foregrounding the issues of racism and labor market segmentation on class, gender and racial lines. The trigger for these ruminations was my presence at a 'million strong' gathering at Taksim Square Istanbul celebrating May Day, an event I subsequently commented on as guest, with

Shahrzad Mojab of the University of Toronto, in an inaugural program of a Kurdish owned, internet-streamed television station.

The issue of racism recurs throughout most of the chapters that follow where I first discuss the issue of Migration in the Mediterranean with its implications for ethnic and religious conviviality taking into account the unequal power relations underwritten by what is often referred to as 'intercultural-dialogue.' I then move on to discuss the complexities associated with Arab and Muslim youth in an attempt to discuss some of the misrepresentations that abound in Western circles. This leads to a discussion of the role played by digitally savvy Arab youth in the recent Arab uprisings predicated on the quest for basic human dignity: Ben Ali's investment, in Tunisia, in widespread ICT provision partly proved his undoing as he was hoisted by his own petard. Together with Linda Herrera, I highlight, apart from the quest for human dignity, civil liberties and democracy, the clamour for jobs in the Middle East and North African (MENA) regions hit by massive unemployment. Unemployment and precarious living remain the themes of the subsequent chapters which focus on the *indignados* in Europe with regard to their protests, in addition to student protests concerning university reform. I conclude by looking at the role of education and the contribution it can make to address the UN Millennium development goals, bearing in mind that education should not be romanticized and should not be accorded powers it does not have. It is not an independent variable.

By way of conclusion to the volume, centering throughout on imperialism, decolonizing strategies and a critique of neoliberalism, I examine the potential of critical pedagogy and a broader critical education for an alternative discourse in educational, cultural and other social activism. I specifically address issues touched on earlier such as the state and neoliberalism (as manifest through the dominant discourse on lifelong learning where I argue for an alternative rendering of this concept). I also discuss Racism and Higher Education and conclude by highlighting, through a brief overview, the major contributions of a select and by no means exhaustive group of exponents of critical pedagogy and a critical education in general.

This book would not have been possible without the encouragement and promptings of a number of friends: Lind Herrera and Antonia Darder (I wrote a piece with each); the late M. Kazim Bacchus and my university colleague, Vincent Caruana who provided me with insights regarding the challenges posed by the United Nation's Millennium Development Goals (MDGs); my former Dean, close friend and co-author, Carmel Borg who nominated me, in 2005, to chair a pre-CHOGM meeting of NGOs concerning education and the MDGs; graduate students with whom I had the pleasure to work at Bogazici University Istanbul, who encouraged me to participate in the May Day celebrations in their city last year (2011) and who invited me to discuss the event on IMC TV; Patrizia Morgante and Loris Viviani from Rome and Seville respectively who filled me in, with valuable information, on events in Rome and Palma de Majorca with regard to the 'occupy' protests; Magda Trantallidi, Dimitris Cosmidis and Maria Nikolakaki from Greece who kept me abreast with events concerning the debtocracy in their country; finally Henry A. Giroux, Victoria Harper and Leslie Thatcher of *Truthout* and Jeffrey St. Clair of *Counterpunch* who helped me place many of my ideas in the public domain. Henry Giroux has been serving as a role model through his work as a public intellectual. I also owe gratitude to my university colleagues Ivan Callus, from the Department of English, University of Malta, for giving me feedback on the entire volume, and Ronald Sultana, Mary Darmanin and Carmel Borg, from my university department with whom I discussed some of these issues. The same applies to Leona English from St Francis Xavier University, Antigonish, Canada, with whom I developed a few of the ideas when we wrote a book together. I must also mention my long time friend and colleague, Godfrey Baldacchino from the University of Prince Edward Island, who provided encouraging comments on some of the chapters when they appeared in their earlier versions as opinion columns in the above outlets. Any remaining shortcomings are my responsibility.

I

Neoliberalism and the State[1]

Neoliberalism has wrought havoc in different areas of social life, not the least of which in health and education. One of the greatest myths promoted by neoliberals is that the nation state is not and should no longer be the main force in those domains – everything should be left to the market. Health care education, infrastructure (financial and legal, as well as physical), and the environment are no longer public goods in this worldview, but rather commodities to be bought and sold. Deregulation has been used to expedite this process and, yet, the credit crunch revealed the hypocrisy and impossibility of such a strategy when national states were forced to intervene, bailing out banks and other institutions to prevent the collapse of the real economy as well as the financial sector. So much for the minimal state! It is an opportune moment to look at the function of the state and assess its role within the contemporary scenario of hegemonic global-ization.

The state provides the conditions for the accumulation of capital through its institutions. Education and training, therefore, have an important role to play, more now than ever, when education to train workers for positions in the economy, including adult learning for work, is said to perform a crucial role in attracting and maintaining investment. In the post-war (WWII) period, a welfare notion of state provision of, for instance, education, prevailed as part of 'the new deal.' This deal was seen by many as a concession by capital to labor. It was also seen within labor politics as very much the result of the struggle for better living conditions by the working class and its represen-tatives.

Neoliberalism

While the state and its bureaucracy continues to retain responsibility for much that had previously been attributed to it, things have changed considerably in recent years. With the onset of neoliberalism, and therefore the ideology of the marketplace, the state has lost its welfare outlook even as it plays a crucial role in terms of providing a regulatory framework for 'the market's' operation.

The neoliberal state has a set of important roles to play. It provides the infrastructure for the mobility of capital, including investment in 'human resource development,' as well as the promotion of an 'employability-oriented,' lifelong, learning policy, although the onus of taking advantage of these 'opportunities' is often placed on the individual or group, often at considerable expense. We witness a curtailment of socially-oriented programs in favor of a market-oriented notion of economic viability, also characterized by public financing of private needs. Public funds are channeled into areas of educational and other activities that generate profits in the private sector. Furthermore, attempts are being made all over the world to leave as little as possible to the vagaries of state agencies and the personnel who work inside them since the state has never been monolithic. Whatever the policies, there are always bureaucratic procedures and 'tried and tested' ways of working, as well as people working inside these agencies, like critical educators in public schools, who are driven by a vision of doing things that may run contrary to what policy makers desire or simply fall short of when delivering established policies. Standardization, league tables, classifications, accountability measures and, more recently, harmonization are some of the means used to bring these institutions and the persons who work inside them in line with the dominant trends and policies. The objective is to render agencies of the state, or that work in tandem with the state through a loose network (a process of governance rather than government), more accountable, more subject to surveillance, and ultimately, more rationalized. And as indicated at the very beginning, the state has no qualms about its role in bailing out banks and other institutions of capital when there is a crisis. As the Brazilian educator Paulo Freire put it so clearly years before the recent credit crunch (he died in 1997):

> Fatalism is only understood by power and by the dominant classes when it interests them. If there is hunger, unemployment, lack of housing, health and schools, they proclaim that this is a universal trend and so be it! But when the stock market falls in a country far away and we have to tighten up our belts, or if a private national bank has internal problems due to the inability of its directors or owners, the state immediately intervenes to 'save them.' In this case, the 'natural,' 'inexorable,' is simply put aside.[2]

The state is very much present in many ways, a point that needs to be kept in mind when discussing any other form of program that conveys the corporate business agenda. We must guard against the widespread neoliberal myth that the state is playing a secondary role in the present intensification of globalization. Capitalism has, since its inception, been globalizing with the active collaboration of nation states (also more recently via the WTO, NAFTA ...), and what we have now is the intensification of this process through information technology where everything occurs in real time. Capitalism as a global system requires national organizations to ensure the internationalization of its manner of production.[3]

The state organizes, regulates, 'educates,' creates and sustains markets, provides surveillance, evaluates, legitimates, forges networks and represses. One should not downplay the role of the repression realized by the state during this period. Behind the whole facade of securing consent (the ideas it helps generate through its institutions, the media etc, enable it to win over popular consent), lurks naked power which, in Mao's famous words, ultimately lies in 'the barrel of a gun.' The state consists of and acts in concert with institutions, such as the media, that provide the climate for acceptance of its policies. Consent is, thus, manufactured. The state, however, also holds a monopoly over the forces of repression such as the police force, the army, wardens, security officers (although the task is often subcontracted to private firms) etc. The state provides a policing force for those who are the victims of neoliberal policies as well as of the related 'structural adjustment programs' in the majority world (I will discuss this in Chapter 11). These victims include blacks, latino/as and the rest of what has been described as the 'human waste disposal sector.'[4] Prisons, and privatized ones at that, have risen in the USA in the emergence of what Henry A. Giroux calls the 'carceral state.'

The prison metaphor can be applied on a larger scale to incorporate migrants from sub-Saharan Africa knocking at the gates of 'Fortress Europe.' Carceral states await the victims of neoliberal policies worldwide, notably in countries that are serving as 'first port of call' for immigrants from Africa and Asia fleeing poverty, starvation (exacerbated by structural adjustment programs), the droughts emanating from climate change and internal wars fueled by a potent Western-based arms industry (the US is the major exporter of arms). The carceral settings awaiting such hapless victims include detention centers (closed centers) where immigrants are kept for long periods prior to decisions being taken regarding whether they should be allowed in as refugees or repatriated. And such a carceral ordeal is experienced on top of the terrible and often tragic experiences of crossing huge tracts of land and desert in the world's largest continent and of risking life and limb crossing from the shores of North Africa in small and hardly durable dinghies and other 'rickety' vessels. A similar ordeal is experienced by Latinos/as attempting to cross *la frontera* (the borderland between Latin America and the USA).

The carceral function of the state with its manifestly repressive orientation, but not without its dose of ideological support, serves to remind us that there is no 100 per cent ideologically pure state apparatus and no 100 per cent purely repressive state apparatus, the difference sometimes being one of degree. Authors like the French philosopher Louis Althusser had singled out the school as being the state's most important ideological apparatus. However, one would have to point to the media as the most influential ideological apparatus, that is, the apparatus that influences minds and helps develop perceptions and manufacture consent in this day and age. And the link between the state and the media has been underscored time and time again by various commentators of a critical bent.

There has been talk of 'media spectacles,' which have come to dominate news coverage and deviate public attention from substantial public issues.[5] Media politics play a crucial role in advancing foreign policy agendas and militarism. Political forces such as al-Qaeda and, in the recent past, the Bush administration, constructed and developed media spectacles to advance their politics. The link between the state and the corporate media during the period of Republican US government under George W. Bush has been established.[6] In this regard, therefore, critical media literacy becomes an important feature of any effective educational experience in this day and age. And the challenge to state-induced media constructions lies within such a type of critical literacy as well as in learning to create and promote an alternative media discourse such as those circulated via YouTube, Twitter, and a variety of web sites. These have a role to play in an alternative progressive discourse in this day and age. Electronic networking has opened up a variety of spaces in this regard. More than this, however, critical media literacy opens a vast and important dimension to the meaning of critical literacy: reading not only the word, but also the world, in Paulo Freire's terms, and I would add, reading the construction of the world via the media.

Althusser seems to be right on target in his pointing to there being no 100 per cent ideological state apparatus. Education has always had a very strong repressive function; this is even more true today. Witness the US high school model with armed security guards making their presence felt in a heavy-handed manner.[7] Other theorists and writers talk of the connections among the state and those institutions we commonly consider neutral, but which – however apparently autonomous – tend to generate the basis for consensus regarding the current state of affairs.[8] They work closely with the state. Some have argued that they serve to prop up the state and that one cannot challenge the state frontally in Western society – see the failure of several head-on, gung-ho revolutions in the twentieth century, including the attacks on the state by Italy's Red Brigades or by Germany's Baader Meinhof (Red Army Faction). For the state to change, work has to be carried out on a large scale and within the inter-stices of these institutions which include the media, law, religion, education, the entertainment sectors, the arts, scientific communities etc. There is a long process of transformation to be effected, which involves work among these institutions that surround and prop up the state. And there invariably arises a struggle for hegemony.

Hegemony is an ancient Greek word. It has been described as a 'social condition in which all aspects of social reality are dominated by or supportive of a single class' or group.[9] It concerns ideas and an entire set of practices and expectations.[10] Opinion leaders and organizers strategically located in different sectors of society play a great part in legitimizing the current state of affairs. Similarly, any movement for change must also operate in the domain of influencing minds and practices. This is intellectual work, with the term 'intellectual' being used not in its elitist sense, but in the sense of people who influence opinions and ways of living, acting etc. This is what progressive social movements partly seek to accomplish in their all-pervasive work.

This theorization of the state, an 'integral state,'[11] has affinities (despite a strong political-ideological difference) with some of the modern managerial technical-rational conceptions of the state with regard to policy formulation and action. The state and its agencies are nowadays said to work not alone, but within a loose network of agencies – governance rather than government. It has also been pointed out that the state further engages in economic activities, which are not left totally in the hands of private industry. In the first place, industry often collaborates in policy formulation in tandem or in a loose network with the state just as some NGOs or labor unions do, the latter often being co-opted in the process into a form of corporatism: they establish and pursue formal and informal links, in and outside the legislature, with key state agents to advance their specific interests.[12] Nowhere is the role of the state as economic player more evident that in higher education (see Chapter 7). The division between public and private becomes blurred. So-called 'public universities' are exhorted to provide services governed by the market and which have a strong commercial basis.

Furthermore, the state engages actively through direct and indirect means, sometimes including a series of incentives. It does this to create a higher education competitive market as part of the 'competition' state – it helps foster competition between different entities as part of sustaining a market in this and other fields, all in keeping with the neoliberal ideology. In short, the state is an active player and has not gone away. It is central to the neoliberal scenario and we underestimate its centrality at our peril!

2

Born Under a Bad Sign: Neoliberalism and the Two September 11s[1]

September of the previous year (2011) led to several reflections on the significance of the 10th anniversary of the 9/11, 2001 attacks on the Twin Towers and the Pentagon.[2] This is as it should be. The memories of the several victims of this dastardly attack demand this.

Equally appropriate were many columns appearing in various outlets reflecting on the policies adopted by the USA in the aftermath of these attacks and the extent to which they suited a culture of militarization, civil repression and consumerism. Obscured because of the particular connotation this date has acquired is the memory of another September 11 which connects with some of the policies decried by many in the aftermath of the New York and Washington attacks – the Chilean coup d'état led by the late Augusto Pinochet against the democratically elected government of Salvador Allende in 1973.

Monday 11 September 2011 marked the thirty-eighth anniversary of this bloody coup which paved the way, and is said to have been deliberately staged to pave the way, for the introduction of the very same neoliberal reforms that, later at a global level, are shown to have benefited from the measures adopted post 9/11/2001.

That attack on the presidential palace in Santiago, Chile, of Tuesday September 11 1973[3] brought an end to one of the longest parliamentary democracies in the region and paved the way for the policies and blueprints developed by the 'Chicago Boys,' Chilean economists, who were sold on Milton Friedman's and Arnold Harberge's principles, to start being implemented against the backdrop of a reign of fascist terror. This reign led to the execution of thousands of declared or suspected leftists. Among the victims were intellectuals such as the musician and folk singer, Victor Jara, killed by death squads in a sports stadium that is now named after him. The national football stadium (not the one where Jara was executed), which was to host a qualification decider for the 1974 World Cup (football), between Chile and the USSR, served as a concentration camp where people were interrogated, tortured or threatened to be shot. The USSR did not turn up for the qualifier affirming its refusal to play on a field associated with events leading to the demise of several victims of the military regime, thus granting Chile an automatic qualification to the W. Germany World Cup.

Thousands were killed, tortured or simply 'disappeared' in the first months of the regime. Survivors such as UK citizen and medical doctor Sheila Cassidy spoke of the horrors of torture carried out by DINA, the Chilean secret police. This is a common feature of situations bearing the stamp of the Monroe Doctrine meant to protect US 'security' and economic interests in the region. The Chile coup was to be followed by other equally terrible coups leading to similar situations of terror such as that in Argentina which led to several arrests, killings and disappearances and that in Turkey in 1980 (like the Argentinean *Madres* movement in Buenos Aires,[4] a Saturday Mothers' movement still makes its presence felt in a central square in Istanbul). These events constituted the bloody prelude to the onset of US driven neoliberal policies in these countries – policies which are liberal only insofar as market economics are concerned but which sit comfortably with a range of fascist conservative policies that lead to clamp downs on any form of dissidence and critical thinking.

In many respects, the notion of a 'September 11' is inextricably linked with the onset of neoliberal policies, ushered in Chile as a form of 'trial run' against the backdrop of a bloody fascist deposition of a democratically elected government. It is also inextricably linked with those very same neoliberal policies that were attacked, on the same date but different year, by Muslim fundamentalists in a manner that shows that the reaction to neoliberalism and hegemonic globalization stems not always from progressive leftists (for example the *Ejercito Zapatista* in Chiapas on 1 January 1994, marking the coming into effect of NAFTA) but also from religious fundamentalists such as Al Qaeda.

Deaths, torture and destruction are a common feature of the post September 11 aftermaths. This is what the Pinochet regime would mainly be remembered for despite any economic growth the country might have registered in terms of its neoliberal capitalist development. While the deaths of thousands of innocent people will also be remembered with respect to the 2001 Twin Towers and Pentagon attacks, we must remember the other forms of destruction, torture and deaths caused in the aftermath against an innocent people in Iraq. To date, there have been no proven connections between this country and the movement that gave rise to the attacks inside the USA. Likewise there has been no incontrovertible proof of this country's alleged possession of WMDs. As with Chile, economic considerations involving the trading of blood seem to be the overriding motive. The notorious Abu Ghraib, Guantanamo Bay and Villa Grimaldi (Santiago) centers stand as stark, chilling reminders of these nefarious policies.

The range of deaths and destruction becomes even broader when we consider that the war has been waged on both fronts, both the foreign and home fronts, in the sense that the debts incurred as a result of the war in Iraq have led to cutbacks in essential services for the poor and needy in the US who are left to flounder by the wayside or end up either in body-bags, having no choice but to fight on the foreign front, or else as inmates in the ever booming private prison industry.[5]

Recent reflections on September 11 lead us to focus on what is valued in society, who is deemed worthy of living or being disposed of, what is it that is fundamentally unsavory about Western imperialist politics and what is it that breeds so much resentment against Western imperialist powers in many parts of the world to lead to such a barbarous and callous attack on ordinary civilians as happened on that particular day in 2001. But it should lead us to reflect on the earlier September 11 and what it represents in terms of the way Western economic interests are safeguarded at the expense of so many innocent lives as was the case in Chile, with the creation of the right (if you can excuse the pun) conditions (toppling an elected government which had been nationalizing services), and the rest of what we call the 'majority world' including Africa, Asia and Latin America – the tri-continental world.

These infamous September 11s and their immediate aftermaths lead us to reflect on how critical thinking, dissent and the construction of plausible democratic alternatives become the first casualties in these situations – when economic interests, at the expense of human rights, occupy centre stage in the foreign policies of Western nations. I am sure that critical thinking, dissent and the construction of plausible democratic alternatives figured in the dreams and narratives of the many persons, young and old (including high school children in Argentina during the 'night of the pencils'), who disappeared and lost their lives in Chile, Argentina and later East Timor and Turkey. This makes a mockery of the exaltation of these very same democratic virtues in these western nations' discourses regarding the basis of a democratic education.

The connection between the Pinochet regime and the destruction of any semblance of a democratic education was reinforced this year as a result of massive student protests in Chile which earned the support of other sectors of the population.[6] The Chilean coup d'état brought to an end not only a long democratic tradition in the country but also the idea of education as a human right. At all levels, including state provision at elementary and secondary schooling, education was rendered a consumer good and has remained so till the time of writing. Students together with a host of other sectors of society, social organizations and trade unions, such as the Central Unitaria de Trabajadores de Chile (CUT), have come together to clamor for the right to a free education in a country where one must pay for public education and where university fees are quite steep, leading families into huge debts, legacies of the neoliberal restructuring occurring since the time of the Pinochet dictatorship. Chilean students have been clamoring for an end to this most undemocratic of measures calling for the right of every citizen to an education, irrespective of means, to be enshrined in the constitution and therefore putting an end to a shameful legacy of the Pinochet rule. Fancy, having to pay for state sponsored elementary and secondary education! This represents the case of stretching the neoliberal thinking with regard to service provision to its extreme. Not that other countries fare much better since any free provision is often poor, underfunded and often of despicable quality which renders the whole issue of choice into a farce. Either pay or be fobbed off with a poor quality service. In the next chapter, Antonia Darder and I will contrast this approach to service provision with an equally radical one (radical can be both right and left with neoliberalism in the form of Thatcherism or Reaganomics being dubbed 'radical') from the same region (Latin America and the Caribbean). This is the Cuban experience which, has had its problems and contradictions, but which is worth viewing if only for the solidity of its principles, allowing for the fact that the actual implementation is the subject of much discussion and controversy.

3

The Promise of Cuba and its Postcolonial Principles[1] – with Antonia Darder

For more than 50 years, Cuba has been one of the most maligned countries in the Western press. As the island's political system grappled with its limitations and shortcomings, as all countries do, mainstream press coverage demonized the island, despite no tangible military threat to the US today. The media continues to justify an obscene economic and political embargo, appeasing a heavily influential right-wing political lobby. In some ways, the geopolitical tensions faced by Cuba's people are not unlike those of Palestinians struggling for economic self-sufficiency and an unalienable right to a homeland.

Yet calls for an end to the blockade stem from different quarters, including the UN, together with various resolutions focused on Palestinians' rights, and the late Pope John Paul II, who denounced the blockade, in no uncertain terms, during his historic visit to Cuba in 1998. We anticipated similar calls when his successor Pope Benedict XVI visited the country this March (2012), a visit which once again placed Cuba in the spotlight. The 1998 visit of Pope John Paul II placed Cuba at the centre of televised debates on the virtues and shortcomings of the revolutionary legacy in this country and their ramifications for the rest of Latin America (it now includes one booming and emerging strong economy, that of Brazil). Earlier appeals to an end to the blockade, however, have fallen on deaf ears. This is undoubtedly linked to strength of counter lobbies and organizations, working against a Palestinian state and an end to the Cuban blockade, who are deeply embedded in the US's internal political firmament. As such, U.S. politicians and political leaders like Barack Obama ignore these lobbies at their peril, tantamount to political suicide; his pandering to the Jewish vote during the campaign trail, with assurances concerning the state of Israel, is indicative of this concern on a prospective President's mind.

The constant demonization of Cuba and its revolution serve to underplay the achievements of a country that captured the imagination of the world on January 1, 1959, when revolutionaries waged the first successful campaign against a western-backed dictatorship (six years after a failed attempt on the Moncada Barracks) in the region. Their successful overthrow of the corrupt Batista regime and subsequent nationalization of assets, many of which were US assets, were a serious affront to 'Yankee imperialism.' The Cuban revolution also brought to an end the use of the island as the financial and recreational playground of affluent US citizens and wealthy investors, severing Cuba's informal role as another U.S. colony; a relationship influenced, once again, by the foreign economic policies of the Monroe Doctrine. This political change also confirmed that an alternative model could emerge from a region that had hitherto only known a colonizing model of governance, which had kept most of its inhabitants economically and politically disempowered.

A Tricontinental Vision

It is not surprising then that the Cuban revolution served as a promising source of real hope not only to the impoverished people of Latin America but also to the rest of the Tricontinental World, to use a term favored by the revolution's tenacious and charismatic architect, Fidel Castro. The term was used in 1960 during a visit to the UN and subsequently Harlem in NYC, where connections were made between the Cuban condition and that of Afro-Americans, considered the most oppressed U.S. population at that time. The plight of Afro-Americans was very evident in Harlem, where the Cuban delegation stayed[2] courtesy of the efforts of Malcolm X among others.[3] A Tricontinental Conference was later held in Havana in 1966. It offered a militant version of the 'Third World' alliance against continued western imperialist designs, an alliance that owes its origins to the Bandung Conference, which had taken place eleven years earlier.[4] The term 'tricontinental' captured a significant feature of the Cuban revolution – its 'South-to-South' international ethos of cooperation and solidarity. Moreover, Castro's notion of 'tricontinental' applied to those who Frantz Fanon had called the 'wretched of the earth' to refer to the exploited and colonized populations of Latin America, Asia and Africa.

But this radical vision of 'tricontinental' was not merely determined by geographical boundaries. If anything, the Cuban delegation's efforts to link with Afro-Americans and their leaders suggest otherwise. Castro and his collaborators, including Ernesto 'Che' Guevara, were fully conscious of the existence of the 'third world' in the 'first world.' Castro remained true to this commitment; even as recently as 2004, he offered help to the 'wretched and oppressed' of the same country that has been the main cause of hardships endured by the Cuban population. These oppressed Americans are the impoverished of New Orleans, a region understood by Cubans as the home of jazz and blues – the soulful music of the oppressed.

Hence, it is not surprising that the woes of impoverished Americans were thrown into sharp relief for Cubans in the aftermath of Hurricane Katrina. True to form, Castro offered to provide access to Cuba's never ending supply of top-notch doctors and health workers to assist with the plight of the poor whose home and communities had been devastated by the storm. Some interpreted the humanitarian gesture as Castro's ultimate insult to his mighty neighbor; and indeed US leaders must have regarded it so, promptly, flatly, and churlishly refusing the offer. Nevertheless, the island's willingness to lend assistance shed light on Cuba's commitment to alleviate poverty and support the oppressed and impoverished anywhere, irrespective of the contentious relations that have existed for decades with the U.S. It also signaled Cuba's commitment to the global south, defined widely. The poor and forsaken of New Orleans, themselves victims of a US war fought on two fronts – an expensive war against the Iraqis to retain geopolitical control in the region and a devastating domestic class war against those of modest means by implementing simultaneous cutbacks of social welfare programs for the needy, while simultaneously providing huge financial bailouts for the wealthy – are embraced as members of this global South.

Impact of Tensions in the Region

The fact that Cuba received much bad press in the Western media is hardly news given the revolution's disruption of the status quo, with respect to both material wealth and power at home and the larger geopolitics of the region. Indeed the isolationist reaction of the US and its blockade against Cuba led the revolutionary Cuban government to the only alternative path available within the cold war scenario of the time. Cuba moved into the Soviet Union's orbit becoming a potential menace to the US, given its geographical location – a situation that would come to a head with the Cuban missile crisis in 1962. The blockade and fomenting of counter-revolutionary attacks such as the *Bahia de los Cochinos* (Bay of Pigs) fiasco, as we would see later with the Contra war in Nicaragua, served to make the revolutionary state more autocratic in its efforts to weed out any possible attempts at sabotage from within and without (not to mention attempts on Castro's life).

Hence the growing tensions in the region offered the Western media a field day, as if being in the USSR's orbit was not reason enough for portraying Cuba in a bad light. Yet, when making this point, we should not deny what leftist colleagues who visited the archipelago referred to as the persistent feeling of repression. Revolutionary movements cannot rest on their laurels especially at a time when a younger generation has emerged with little remembrance of life in Cuba under the former dictatorship. Whatever the achievements of the revolution, probably lost on the younger generation and those who think the country must 'kick on' and not cling to the past, there is a need to ensure a plausible system of democracy that convinces one and all that the Cuban government has the backing of the people, whatever form democracy might take. We say this to emphasize, despite the rhetoric, that Western style bourgeois representative democracy is not the only conceivable model of democracy and as the current financial collapse shows, it has its limitations. These limitations are constantly being underlined by the *indignados* in Spain and Greece and elsewhere, as references to the emergence of more capillary forms of power and grassroots democratic networking abound.[5]

At this juncture, it is also helpful to recall that the Sandinistas in Nicaragua (as we shall see in the next chapter) legitimized their leadership following the overthrow of a corrupt dictatorship in 1979 with an internationally monitored election, which they won by a landslide in the early eighties – a democratic process that the U.S. refused to honor. This points to the simple fact that whatever model is adopted, the process of democracy must be genuine rather than a case of mass manipulation and intimidation, which has resulted in certain forms of 'direct democracy' being denounced, when put into practice elsewhere.

Currently, Cuba's policy of exerting strict control over departures and arrivals of citizens from abroad also needs to be revised, given that the situation has dramatically changed since the early days of the revolution when Cuba lost a huge percentage of its brainpower, in terms of doctors and other professionals, to the US. If anything, the small nation now engages in an impressive proactive policy of exporting such power. Furthermore, also in need of rethinking is the manner in which serious infringements (i.e. drug trafficking) are uncompromisingly punished by the death penalty. There is no doubt that the use of the death penalty anywhere, including the USA, stirs mixed emotions. As in the recent execution of Troy Davis in Texas, the 1989 execution of Arnaldo Tomas Ochoa Sanchez, a hero of the Angola war, and his associates raised human rights concerns; this was countered by the Cuban concern that it had to avoid being liable to accusations of being some kind of transit centre for drug trafficking, as was the case with Panama, an image which the USA would mercilessly exploit.

Yet, while underlining such strictures, we must also do justice to a country that, much like Nicaragua (although forgiveness even of torturers was a feature of the initial period of the Sandinista revolutionary government), was forced to contend with overwhelming obstacles in its efforts to serve as a revolutionary model to other countries within the US intercontinental sphere of influence in the Americas. Despite sordid moments, the Cuban revolution hoped to evolve into an alternative political economic structure in contestation to the West, where unrelenting capitalist accumulation has functioned to the benefit of the few, at the expense of the many.

One cannot help but underline the potential that lies within the Cuban model, including its health and educational systems, which are the envy of many nations, including the much-heralded countries whose universities lead the 'world rankings.' The *Universidad de la Habana* (University of Havana), although not recognized in the top flight of these university leagues, has a medical school that is considered among the best in the world. Ask the many ambitious students from the formerly Anglo-colonized Caribbean who break their backs learning Spanish in order to gain admission to Cuba's medical school.

The same can be said of a science centre (Cuba has quite a number of them) lauded, in the late 80s, as a remarkable research institution of its kind in a program shown on *Rai* (Italian) TV by that great connoisseur of Latin American affairs, Gianni Minà, editor of the Italian review *Latino America*; Minà had carried out a long televised and published interview with Castro himself. In 2000, Argentina's former soccer superstar Diego Armando Maradona, like others, chose to go to Cuba for rehabilitation from a life-threatening, drug-related illness.

Cuba today places its educational and medical facilities at the service of not only its own people and celebrities but also the common people of Africa, Asia and many other parts of the world. As part of its revolutionary commitment to international cooperation, with no strings attached – quite credible now that the connection with the dismantled USSR is history and a small country such as Cuba cannot harbor imperial designs – Cuba makes the products of these institutions (teachers, health workers, doctors) available for export against token fees, depending on the receiving country's ability to pay. It is, in fact, the bilateral, trilateral or multilateral agreements generated by these forms of collaborations with other countries, within the context of South-to-South cooperation, which is the primary focus of a forthcoming book.[6]

South-to-South Relations

This notion of horizontal South-to-South relations is contrasted with the more global and dominant models of hierarchical North-South relations, which keep former colonies even today in a colonial bind. Different organizations of an international nature are also important to this process. In addition, we now have the European Union joining the act with its EuropeAid programs, although it is to be said that the EU is not monolithic and contains spaces where people, well aware of the history of USAID, for instance, use their influence in working groups and other EU epistemic communities to help develop more reciprocal forms of relations with 'developing' countries. EU involvement requires studies of the kind carried out, in this new book, with regard to the older and more well known forms of North-to-South aid. We now also have the Union of the Mediterranean, propelled by France's Sarkozy with the support of Spain's Zapatero, which also involves North-to-South relations in a regional context. Of course, it remains to be seen what consequences the current 'debtocracies' in Southern European countries will have on such a project.

Whatever the case, the South-to-South relations, consistently promoted by Cuba even in its most difficult economic restructuring days post-1990 and at the time of the US decision (still not revoked) to boycott any firm that engages in commercial relations with the Caribbean island, is presented as an alternative model for international exchange. This model is based not on predominantly business interests or financial profit, which would render it consistently subject to 'bottom line' considerations, but instead on the revolutionary humanist principle of communal sharing. Rather than being regarded as the individual rights of a few, the world's assets are viewed as the birthright of humankind.

In a 'delinking' process, Southern assets can be exchanged in a complementary manner. Venezuelan oil at low prices and interest rates is exchanged for Cuban teachers, doctors and health workers. Cuba had Venezuelan literacy tutors trained in the 'Yo si Puedo' pedagogical method created by Cuban educator Leonela Realy. As a result, Cuba helped the Venezuelan government keep the Bolivarian revolutionary momentum going by teaching one and a half million people to read and write.[7] This satisfied a great social demand. It was then followed by an attempt to articulate the achievements of the crusade with the formal, technical-rational demands of a state educational system that is crucial to Venezuela's development.[8] In this way, Southern assets can also be shared to enable traditionally subordinated people and countries to delink from the structural residues of their colonial past. However, this process is not without its critics. There are those who have expressed civil rights concerns as to whether qualified personnel chosen for these exchanges have the option to decline work assignments abroad.

Beyond Romanticizing Cuba

Truly, Cuba is not to be romanticized. Great poverty exists. Prostitution, for example, that very same social predicament of exploited poor women and adolescent girls initially tackled head on by the revolutionary government through educational and rehabilitation measures such as schools for prostitutes, is on the rise once again, especially in tourist areas (similar to other countries), despite its illegality. There is also an overproduction of qualified people without reciprocal economic investments to integrate them. Should this be solely blamed on the infamous blockade – which certainly has no justification today (if ever), now that the Soviet 'threat' to the USA has been nullified?

Raul Castro was recently on record stating that one cannot blame the country's economic ills only on the blockade. There is a lot of work to be done in the economic sector and this should be the sort of challenge to which the country can rise. It has, after all, overachieved in many other fields (sport, medicine, science, education), and has an enviable environmental track record. According to a 2006 WWF (World Wildlife Federation) report, Cuba is the *only* country in the world with sustainable development.[9] It combined high human development standards (high literacy and health indexes) with a low ecological footprint; this includes the rate of electricity consumed and carbon dioxide emitted per capita.[10]

The blockade has been condemned by several world figures; and one must not lose sight of the fact that one of them, the late Pope John Paul II, was himself a staunch opponent of Soviet communism and widely perceived to have been a catalyst for its overthrow. Maybe the real threat to the US and its unbridled market economy stems from something else. If left to freely develop its socialist vision of democracy, Cuba might serve as a credible and more viable alternative to US-led capitalism. Now that Cuba has modified some of its old and perhaps ossified ways, even cultivating market-socialism, we might want to consider whether the country has the potential today to meets it early promise and truly develop – through its *capacity to share*,[11] with no strings attached – into a microcosm of another world that is possible.

In the next chapter, I take a look at another revolutionary experiment in the same region which provided insights for an antidote to neoliberalism in a number of spheres including health and education. Alas, as with the revolution in Grenada, this revolutionary experiment, while capturing the imagination of many people throughout the world, many of whom flocked to the country to lend their support, both material and moral, fizzled out over time. The memories of all that was exciting and innovative, at least in conception – though perhaps not always in implementation – live on and can still inspire, in my view.

4

Nicaragua Three Decades On

An earlier draft of this chapter was written for and published in *Truthout* in the Fall of 2010.[1] It was meant to mark what was then the 30th anniversary of a mass literacy crusade that had captured the imagination of several people ensconced in several parts of the world. The country in question was the Central American state of Nicaragua and the crusade occurred a year after a revolutionary movement wrested power from the grasp of a dictatorial regime and its oligarchy. This 1979 revolution attracted several people from different parts of the world, many declaring themselves as internationalists. They arrived in Managua and other places in droves, from Canada, the US, Spain, Ireland, the UK ... There was hope. People who believed in an alternative world were willing to contribute to the development of a revolutionary Nicaragua. The country's people, or rather the majority of them, led by a revolutionary group, had stood up to the might of the United States, the dominant power in the region. A change had finally come!

And yet attempts were made, as with the Cuban revolution, to destabilize the revolution through what was known as the Contra War – counterrevolutionary forces who often wreaked havoc with their sorties from neighboring Honduras. There were deaths throughout the eighties. They involved peasants, popular educators, health workers and engineers. One of them, Benjamin Linder, an American engineer, was killed in 1987 (while controversy over the funding of Contras was raging in the USA) while working on a hydroelectric dam in the rural North. Yet the earlier deaths did not deter the government, democratically elected in the early 80s, from carrying out what came across as an innovative health and education program. The literacy crusade, coordinated by Jesuit priest Fernando Cardenal, was probably the highlight of the educational reforms. It was intended to provide people with what they craved – free quality education and health. It did more than this. The crusade helped keep the revolutionary momentum going. Everyone and everything was on the go. A large scale 'offensive' was carried out against illiteracy. In a conception that stretches my imagination to recall Shakespeare's final 'reconciliation plays' (see *The Winter's Tale*), people from the city, who had the advantage of a good formal education and were, therefore, likely to play a role in future as the governing political class, were sent to the rural areas to live with and learn from the peasants while also teaching them literacy. At least, with regard to the overall conception, if not its execution, this was a wonderful idea – forging a 'national popular' unity, bringing together 'town' and 'country,' with people from each side learning from each other. While professionals were welcome and had important roles to play, they were encouraged to work in concert with members of the community. This was very much the case in the health sector where health popular educators were engaged. One such popular educator is Maria Hamlyn Zuniga, herself a friend of the late Benjamin Linder. I interviewed her twice, the first time the year I met her in Toronto (1990)[2] and the second time in 2005[3]. This is what she had to say about the Nicaraguan popular education program:

> Popular education was fundamental to the transformation from a dictatorship to a new society based on equality and justice for all. At one point, over one third of the Nicaraguan population, over one million people, were involved in some form of education. The formal education from pre-school to adult education was free and universal. There were over 45,000 popular educators involved in carrying out programs in the communities around the country – continuing the efforts of the literacy crusade in spite of the counter-revolu-

tionary war. Informal education was common in every sector, with thousands of persons receiving workshops and education for living in the transition from the dictatorship to a more just and equal society. In health, over 100,000 persons, especially women and youth, were involved in the popular health brigades working on health promotion and prevention in all the municipalities, towns and rural areas of the country. These popular education programs depended, to a large degree, on the generosity and support of international solidarity.[4]

The attempt was to propagate a philosophy of education based on the principles of popular education said to be followed in the Christian-based communities in Brazil and elsewhere, and which were said to have been promoted prior to the overthrow of the dictatorship by Jesuits and their helpers from the University in Central America (UCA) at Managua. It was meant to be a bottom-up, democratic approach to learning, starting from where the people are. This is in keeping with the ideas of Paulo Freire and other popular educators; Freire was, indeed, a consultant to the Nicaraguan literacy campaign.

Granted, overzealousness, inexperience (many of the literacy brigadistas were pupils attending the lycées) and the need to carry out the program in a period of three months made this a far from perfect venture.[5] Some would even go as far as to argue that it represented a travesty of Freirean principles with so-called dialogue taking the form of a mechanistically administered questionnaire. Furthermore, changing the mindset of a people to make their own decisions is quite difficult after years of conditioning that accustomed them to expect directives from above. Prescription was the order of the day in the dictatorial context. This prescription, referred to in education circles, following Freire, as 'Banking Education,' stifles creativity. People begin to 'fear freedom.' As Zuniga argued, based on her own experience in health education in Nicaragua, 'there was always the tendency toward expecting the orientations for the educational programs to come from the Ministry of Health rather than being developed at the local level as a response to the particular situation.'[6] But as far as the underlying ideas go, a wonderful educational and social concept was born or rather reborn. It was all in keeping with the notion of a country roused for transformation.

I say 'reborn' because this campaign echoed a similar effort in the region 20 years or so earlier – the Cuban literacy campaign, referred to in the previous chapter. And it paralleled another simultaneous effort in the Caribbean, that of the New Jewel Movement in Grenada.[7] In fact, there was a strong educational collaboration between the literacy Cruzada on the Atlantic Coast (English literacy in Bluefields) and the Centre for Popular Education (CPE) in Grenada; two literacy volunteers from Grenada worked there.[8] All efforts and especially their sequel, a broader popular education program based on similar pedagogical principles, were the target of saboteurs; the Grenadian one was brutally crushed following the overthrow of the Grenadian revolution. With regard to Nicaragua, once again the Monroe Doctrine, as a result of which the USA is meant to guard this region from the intervention of any European power (the specter of the old Soviet Union loomed large in the context of the Cold War), made its presence felt. The mere mention of Nicaragua – 'the one that got away' during Carter's tenure of office – seemed to be enough to make Reagan see red. This was a revolution that had to be crushed and, as is always the case when a revolutionary popular pedagogy is at the heart of it, the pedagogues involved risk life and limb in going about their teaching. Paulo Freire, for instance, was arrested after the 1964 coup in Brazil because of his pedagogical activities. Popular educators caught teaching literacy in places like Guatemala and El Salvador,[9] in the midst of a civil war, were also deemed subversive and were punished by death. Popular educators caught going about their work by counterrevolutionaries in Nicaragua often suffered the same fate. In a conversation with Freire, the radical American educator Myles Horton recalls his horrific experience of witnessing the corpse of a popular educator with a slit throat.[10] Horton had been an international observer during the Nicaraguan general elections.

The Contra War proved to be the best means of undermining the revolution with the people gradually being worn out. As expected in situations characterized by a civil war, repressive measures had to be taken by a government whose first years in power were, as I indicated in the previous chapter, marked by forgiveness, including the forgiveness of those who were guilty of torture and other callous acts during the dictatorship, unlike the first years of the Cuban revolution,[11] one should remark. Repression also meant banning newspapers like *La Prensa* when suspected of favoring the Contras. Such measures allowed right-wing hacks in the Western media a field day in terms of portraying the Sandinistas in a negative light. The heavy toll in terms of human lives led the people to vote for an end to the war in 1990 – which saw Dona Violeta Chamorro's *UNO* win the elections. Many of the gains of the revolution were gradually lost as structural adjustment programs made their presence felt. The ideals of the revolution and the pedagogical concepts involved in the Literacy campaign of 1980 soon became a thing of the past, only to be savored in the museum dedicated to this effort. The rest is quite a familiar depressing story which Zuniga takes up:

... from 1990 on, the excessive requirements of the Breton Woods institutions has resulted in the total dismantling of the programs of the RPS, including restructuring and privatization under the guise of 'modernization of the health and education sectors.' Nicaragua is among the most highly indebted nations in the world. It has the most severe poverty in Latin America after the regrettable state of Haiti.[12]

What makes the situation even worse is that the Sandinista movement, which derives its name from the popular national hero, Augusto Cesar Sandino, who led a national revolt against the occupying US marine force in the 1930s and which was much later founded by a schoolteacher, Carlos Fonseca Amador, is a pale shadow of its former self – and that is putting it mildly. As Zuniga states, there is polarization in the party, with the group supporting Daniel Ortega, who was president in the first 11 years of the revolution, having 'become part of the new entrepreneurial class, the new oligarchy in Nicaragua, which maintains power and privilege without regard for the poverty and the misery in which the vast majority of the population are living. In part, this is the result of the fact that nobody was prepared for the defeat, the changes and the abuses that followed the fall of the Sandinistas from power in 1990.'[13]

The Sandinistas are accused of having sold out, of having engaged in a pact with the liberal party, which preserves the political status quo. They are no longer perceived as providing a popular alternative and, therefore, as serving as a counter-hegemonic force. And, yet, the legacy of the pedagogical reforms so spectacularly ushered in 31 years ago through the literacy campaign can still be found in the work of NGOs and the work of people in dispersed territories who have kept the flame of revolutionary pedagogical organization alive. From the 'terrible beauty' that was once born, there emerges hope. There is hope in the work of those determined not to allow the forces of neoliberalism to crush those dreams entertained three decades ago. It is opportune, three decades or so later, and at a time when people are seeking responses to hegemonic 'colonial' neoliberal approaches to education, to revive memories of these events, taking into account not only the successes involved, but also the failures. Such memories can trigger the dream of an alternative pedagogy that, in combination with several other comple- mentary efforts (education is not an independent variable; it does not change things on its own), can usher in another world that is possible. Educational efforts such as those belonging to Nicaragua's revolutionary experiences, as well as other efforts in popular education and that repressed area in Western countries known as independent working class education, foreground the notion of national-popular solidarity. One area in which the issue of solidarity has been raised time and time again is that of workers' education and rights. It is to this area that my thought now turns, triggered off by events I witnessed a year ago in Istanbul but which connected with my concerns as an educator and writer focusing on the politics of education and social activism over the years.

5

The Meaning of Workers' Solidarity Today

May 1 celebrations occur in various countries, the USA alas not being one of them, despite its strong historical connections with the labor movement and labor politics. In recent years I have been a frequent visitor to Istanbul in Turkey primarily because of academic commitments. In my most recent visit, I was fortunate to witness a very vigorous celebration[1] in the well known Taksim Square. Over one million people, representing various organizations, ranging from the Turkish Communist Party to unions, the Kurdish party, women's organizations and Islamic socialists, thronged the square. There was also a massive presence of members of the police force in and around the centre as the whole area was cordoned off and people making their way to the demonstration had to go through security checks. The vitality of the whole gathering, enhanced by the strains of invigorating modern music and chants, familiar to those who have experienced the cauldron of a Turkish football stadium on match day, could be felt throughout. A large number of youth and especially young women, many in their teens, made their presence felt. These were youth clamoring for change and an end to corruption and scandals (in the Turkish case there was also a scandal concerning public exams) and of course the issue of precarious living in neoliberal times. These are recurring themes nowadays (as we shall see in the next two chapters) and were certainly addressed in several May Day celebrations around the world. If youth is widely regarded as the symbol of hope for a better world then Taksim Square on May 1st 2011 provided ample evidence of this.

Turkey's celebration of May 1st as International Workers' Day was of particular significance. This was only the third time the celebration was held, following its long ban which was lifted by the government in 2009. In 1977 a similar celebration was marred by fatal violent attacks which left dozens of protesters dead as unknown gunmen opened fire. The victims' names were called out at this year's manifestation by a famous Turkish actor in a poignant moment which brought to mind the country's tragic past – this included a 1980 military coup that is widely believed to have been intended to pave the way for the onset of neoliberalism (shades of Chile seven years earlier) in the country. This point was raised time and again by several of the fine graduate students with whom I had the pleasure to work in the School of Education at the University of the Bosphorous (Bogazici University) in the summer of 2009.

The memory of protests and violence also reminded us of what is going on in the region as part of the struggle for work and dignity, and greater democratic openings. Tunisia, Egypt, Syria, Yemen, Bahrain and Libya would constantly come to mind. The strong presence of Kurds at the Taksim manifestation also served to invoke a concept of democracy in which the rights of minorities are recognized and valorized, a democracy devoid of homogenization and one which affirms social, including ethnic, difference. In Turkey, this May Day was also marked by the launching of a new satellite and web-streamed TV channel (Al-Jazeera style) – IMC TV (imc-tv.com) – which devoted ample coverage of the celebrations and provided discussions from the studio and abroad regarding their significance around the world.

Internationally speaking, this must have been an international May Day celebration that threw into sharp relief the terrible condition in which the working class and déclassé members of the once lower middle classes are living. One speaks nowadays of not simply 'haves' and 'have-nots' but also, as Henry Giroux and others have argued, 'who is deemed to have the right to live' and who is deemed 'disposable' – therefore denied, in the latter case, the right of life. This is a point Giroux constantly makes.[2] He reproduces a very apt line from Judith Butler,[3] namely the question regarding 'which lives count as human and as living, and which do not.' We are certainly living in a period in which many people constitute what the Polish sociologist, Zygmunt Bauman calls the 'human waste disposal' category.[4] Disposable persons were internationally exposed, in the USA, in the aftermath of Hurricane Katrina. Human disposability was underlined in certain provinces and states throughout the world as a result of cutbacks in social spending, for instance spending on public health measures which might well include, as in one documented case in the USA, spending on life-dependant heart transplants. All this is part of an attempt to render the state leaner, a hypocritical attempt, given the way the so-called 'lean' state has bailed out banks and other enterprises in times of fiscal crises, as with the recent credit crunch – which takes us to the opening chapter ...

May Day also raises the issue of the meaning of worker solidarity in this day and age. In this respect, the presence of women and people from different ethnic groups in the Taksim manifestation contrasted with the symbolic images that loomed large on bill boards and banners. The image of a mustached, muscular worker hearkened back to a homogenizing masculine concept of 'the worker': the antiquated images of the sturdy-looking peasant or construction worker. In this respect, a new and more inclusive language and form of representation of work and workers is called for. The figure of Stalin, in the banner of the Turkish Communist Party, also looked ominous. Would this be a case of Jurassic Marxism? It looked out of place among the presence of youth struggling against the trampling over of human rights exemplified by the 1977 tragedy, subsequent banning of May Day celebrations and the infamous military coup. The current economic scenario worldwide evokes socialist thinking and continues to render ludicrous Fukuyama's proclamation of the 'end of history.' One would expect, however, that any notion of socialism being espoused is a creatively forward-looking one, marked by a new language, and not one which hankers after the specific version that Stalin embodied, a version which represents its worst totalitarian, murderous and ossified forms.

On a more international level, the notion of worker solidarity should be one that extends beyond national boundaries and which encompasses the plight of immigrants as well as that of the so-called 'autochthonous' population. When I was invited in 2008 to speak on the significance of Workers' Day at a seminar organized by the largest trade union in my country, I emphasized this aspect of worker solidarity. The kind of worker solidarity called for is an international and not a national one. The latter is very much the hallmark of *National* Socialism with its racist, ethnocentric underpinnings. Readers need no reminding of what this approach perpetrated in 20th century history.

This is one of the greatest challenges facing those committed to a genuinely leftist democratic politics in this region. This involves work of an unmistakably educational nature. And the kind of educational work in which one must engage, in the contemporary context, is a lengthy one. With local working class people, living in a state of precariousness, being the ones most likely to suffer from the devastating effects of neoliberal globalization policies, this work becomes ever so urgent. Unless such an educational strategy is developed, it is more likely that working class people become attracted to the kind of populist right wing and often neo-fascist discourse that plays on their fears and leads to further segmentation and antagonism among workers on ethnic lines. This can result in misplaced alliances and the mystification of the fact that both they and the immigrants share a common fate: that of being oppressed and subaltern. Both are victims of a ruthless process of capitalist exploitation. There have been cases, in certain places, when traditionally socialist parties, once championing the cause of the laboring classes, have been accused of shunning the responsibility of working toward fostering inter-ethnic solidarity among workers. They are accused of doing so for fear of losing electoral votes, a situation which bodes ill for a genuinely democratic politics predicated on worker solidarity across ethnic, national and gender lines.[5]

It is a politics which, as shown by Antonia Darder[6] and others, eschews the kind of identity politics that has led to what the Egyptian writer Nawal El Saadawi[7] calls a postmodern divide and rule, where the totalizing structure of an ever-globalizing capitalism is confronted by a divisive politics among the grassroots. In contrast, Darder's scholarship focuses on the way capitalism serves as a totalizing force, structuring different forms of entities on gender, ethnic, and nationality lines, with class having a transversal presence. Rather than reflecting on 'race' as some biological and essential factor, she focuses, especially in her work with Rodolfo Torres, on racism resulting from the process of racialization that is part and parcel of the imperatives of capitalist production and the manner in which its segmentation of the global labor market occurs.[8]

This situation calls for solidarity across movements and a focus on the totalizing structure of capitalism which, as Darder and others have argued, is predicated on different segmentations as well as environmental pillage. It seems that the various movements throughout North Africa and the Middle East as well as the *indignados* and Occupy movements throughout the USA , Europe and elsewhere seem to be thinking along these lines. The next few chapters focus on this groundswell which is being witnessed across different contexts, starting with recent events in Europe and then moving, following the discussion on immigration and racism, to North Africa and the Middle East.

Politics of Indignation as Rome Burns[1]

The 99 per cent came out in full force in Rome as Italy's capital city joined several other cities on Saturday, 15 October 2011, in serving as a venue for massive protests against the current global economic crisis.

The legitimate concerns of the many (thousands) were overshadowed in the media by the details of violence perpetrated by the few. These concerns at Piazza San Giovanni, in front of the Lateran Basilica, echoed similar concerns being expressed in chants and slogans in the streets and squares of other cities, including no less than 80 cities in Spain, in the context of the plural movement '15M: democracia real ya' (15th May: Real Democracy Now!), and now, prominent globalized venues such as Athens' Syntagma Square (where the Greek Parliament is situated) and besieged Wall Street. They also echoed some of the concerns expressed as part of the Arab uprising in Egypt and Tunisia since the quest for democracy in these two countries should not obscure the fact that there is also an urgent quest for more jobs and decent employment in a region which has among the highest unemployment rates in the world; the unemployment rate hovers around the 25 per cent mark, surpassed only by Sub-Saharan Africa.

Most of the protests were, for the most part, peaceful, taking different forms and involving, in many cases, social media, streets and squares. The violence came from the state's repressive forces, as has been the case in Egypt; Tunisia; other parts of the Arab world (Libya, Syria, Yemen, Bahrain); and the USA. Rome constituted one prominent exception and this leads to a number of questions and considerations. The violence did not come from the vast majority of persons who, in their thousands, converged

on Piazza San Giovanni, a prominent venue for political manifestations, including union manifestations, in Italy. And yet Italian
state TV bulletins went overboard with their coverage of the
violence by a group employing Black Bloc tactics, thus undermining the significance of the mass protest event. The violent
minority group, disavowed by many of the demonstrators, were
identified as anarchists who employ similar tactics in several
manifestations, including the 2001 G8 Genoa Summit.

Conspiracy theories, which have even been floating across
some Italian TV channels, suggest that the thugs certainly acted
in the interest of those who want to maintain the status quo and
who do not want to understand or acknowledge the reasons
behind these manifestations of indignation. This recalls UK
Prime Minister David Cameron's reference to the riots in the UK
as 'criminality pure and simple.' As argued by Sam Mclean, in the
RSA Review, 'Demonising whole communities or groups of
people, taking away social housing and refusing to tackle the root
causes of civil unrest will only serve to deepen the "social
misrecognition" that helps to explain why people feel able to
resort to mass vandalism and violence in their own neigh-
bourhood.'[2]

There were others in Italy who saw the violence as providing
the right pretext to discredit the protest movement, which
consisted of people of different political stripes (party symbols
were at a premium in Rome and other cities such as Palma de
Majorca).[3] It can serve to reinforce the hackneyed view that
protests against neoliberalism predominantly come from the left,
which is frequently presented, in certain media and political
quarters, as having a 'history of violence.' This evokes memories
of 'gli anni di piombo' (the years of lead) in the seventies, never
mind the fact that different carnages – stragi – such as those at
Piazza Fontana in Milan (12 December, 1969) and the Bologna
train station (2nd August, 1980) were attributed to militant right-
wing groups. The protest march in Rome involved people of

different political persuasion, including professors, workers, and others who would normally not participate in these events.

Others can argue that infiltrators, such as those in Rome, represent extreme right-wing elements like those who often make their presence felt in and around Italy's soccer stadia (the so called ULTRAS – soccer fans who create an atmosphere to encourage their teams and intimidate the opposition, often going overboard with their actions which are often influenced by political ideologies – and 'teppisti,' who engage in vandalism, violence, and other disturbances of the public peace), that, on the eve of the 2009 Champions League (football) final held there, earned Rome the appellation in a section of the UK press of 'stab city'; the title now belongs to Limerick in Ireland. They are a sinister straw in the wind. Some of these people would be bent on taking advantage of present disgruntlement and indignation to perpetrate what can at best be termed *squadristi* (violent and often murderous squads of the Fascist period) tactics.

Once again, conspiracy theories can easily emerge. The violence targeted at shops on the Via Cavour and the church at Piazza San Giovanni, in which symbols of Christianity such as a crucifix and a statue of the Madonna were destroyed, can reflect disgruntlement with not only capitalism, but also perceived church-state collusion in Italian politics, especially those of the post-war period. Protests in each locality focus on global issues alongside issues inextricably connected with the local context. Part of the anger in these mass protests was also directed at corruption and the ruling political class as well as at the global market economy.

My interpretations of the violence are simply speculations concerning the actions of what really was a minority group who caught security forces unawares. Some of the police would have been reluctant to risk another Genoa situation (the killing of an activist by a security force member during the G8 summit), also given their 'meager salary,' but many were engaged in scuffles.

Over 100 are said to have suffered injuries in clashes with the thugs. There was also collaboration between the participants and the police.[4]

The Rome experience continues, however, to raise unsettling questions concerning where these events will lead, in the same way that questions are raised about the Arab uprising and its future trajectory. Experiences like those in Rome raise the issue that this current disgruntlement may result in a swing to either the right or left. Lessons from twentieth century history indicate that fascism often thrived on situations of popular disgruntlement and social unrest. Although I do not see this happening at the present time, I would be cautious about any predictions concerning the potential outcomes of these protests, especially in Western societies.

A prominent Italian, Antonio Gramsci, once wrote about 'spontaneity' (*spontaneità*) and 'conscious direction' (*direzione consapevole*). Are these protest gatherings being consciously directed? If not, isn't there the danger that these 'movements' take a trajectory which is much different, in political orientation, from what is being augured by progressives? Alternatively, if the answer to the same question is 'yes,' where is the 'conscious direction' coming from? There are no guarantees in this politics of popular indignation and mobilization.

And, yet, these mobilizations of people, clamoring for greater transparency, meaningful democracy and grassroots partici- pation, nourish hope for the creation of a world in which people are placed before profits and where the public good takes prece- dence over the vagaries of the market. The presence of youth in the Rome manifestation, as elsewhere, indicates the impatience of those who hold out the promise of a better future. Short-changed, rendered déclassé and forced to live a precarious life, they express their indignation toward a situation that cannot persist any longer, uniting in a global chorus of 'Ya Basta!' In Spain, one of the slogans was 'No somos mercancía en manos de políticos y banqueros' (we are not merchandise in the hands of politicians and bankers) – see *El País.com España.*

Youth feature in the various movements represented throughout the world, including such movements as the Via Campesina, present at the forefront of the Rome manifestation. The Via Campesina movement is an international movement, which brings together men and women farmers, small scale agricultural producers, landless peasants, indigenous people, migrants from different parts of the globe and is in favor of small-scale sustainable agricultural production as opposed to transnational and corporate-driven agricultural production. It represents a global movement with a cosmic vision for change concerning southern people, including the dispossessed and landless peoples, who maintain a relationship of respect and harmony with Mother Earth and the oceans.[5] Despite the impossibility of predicting where this will all lead, youngsters whose politically engaged action and vision encompass such larger global dimensions, reflecting a strong sense of international solidarity, constitute significant resources of hope. Youth uprisings against neoliberalism and corporate greed have been widespread. Others have been more specific and have made education the target of their protests. Earlier reference was made to the situation concerning Chilean students who secured allies in fighting for free education as a right which needs to be entrenched in the constitution and activated. Though being university students they are focusing on education in its totality and might well venture into larger issues, forging strong alliances in the process. We cannot overlook, however, the greater struggle for public space in an age of commodification and privatization. And higher education constitutes one specific space of this sort. It is to the struggle to free university as a public space and not to allow it to remain a target of neoliberal reforms that the book now turns.

45

7

University Burns: A View from Europe[1]

There has been much writing on the corporatization of universities and other higher education (HE) institutions in North America. The writing spells out the danger of their conversion into training institutions rather than serving as institutions that take on board the ongoing need to contribute to the generation of a healthy public sphere. Much of what is written, even in these spaces,[2] connects with what is going on in other parts of the world, notably in Europe, not least through the language and guidelines provided by the European Union.

And this state of affairs has been and continues to be contested in many parts of the continent with protests, sit-ins and university occupations. It would not be amiss to regard these actions as an integral part of the many actions, occurring in several European countries, regarding 'debtocracies,' the limits of traditional representative democracy; political corruption; a politics devoid of morality ('morality in politics is only optional' said one prominent former Italian minister); precarious living; and, in the words of one protester in Vienna, a situation whereby 'We will have higher educational degrees than our parents, but we will never attain their standard of living.'[3]

Universities and other HE institutions are by and large being encouraged to undergo a transformation into places for 'entrepreneurship' and to prepare people for jobs. Harmonization processes are being established throughout the European Union, as part of what is known as the Bologna process: an agreement among ministers of education in Bologna to render the systems of Higher Education in different European countries compatible, allowing credit transfer from one place to another. These changes bring with them a series of bureaucratic procedures. This has shifted the balance of power between academia and administration in favor of the latter. Measurement becomes a very important aspect of this situation where quality is judged primarily through the transformation of complex processes into quantitative indicators – everything is judged in terms of easily measured outcomes.

Courses once lauded for their length and depth of analysis have been shortened into credits and are competence based. Academics are meant to be made accountable through compliance with time-consuming bureaucratic procedures. Furthermore, funded research by and large takes on the form of R&D (research and development) and is often evaluated in terms of the amount of money it manages to attract. It must appeal to those who play the tune, often corporate enterprises. Community work is frowned upon or is confined to second- or third-class institutions in a proposed diversified system intended to classify higher education institutions into different leagues. A few, so-called world-class universities are meant to play in the major league. Others are to be content with serving as teaching universities.[4] Still others are some kind of cross-breed in serving as regional universities.

In this proposed scenario, one also observes a possible separation between teaching and research. Privatization is encouraged, and the distinction between private and public is blurred as public funds are often siphoned for private needs. The state helps create, sustain and provide the regulatory framework for markets, including the HE market. It, therefore, encourages competition also in the HE sector, hence the term 'competition state' being used in accounts of this system.[5] This takes us back to Chapter 1 and the discussion on the state.

All this has implications for academics who, in several universities, notably those that will serve as predominantly 'teaching universities,' have to cope with large numbers of students in their classes. They would also have a large teaching load in a process of 'massification' of HE. A small elite is ensconced in 'world class' universities, enjoying all the necessary facilities and assistance for research. Overburdening with teaching often results in few research opportunities and less time for contributions to the public sphere. There is less time for involvement in initiatives providing open access to members of the community, to engage in outreach work within communities and to make other contributions such as writing articles in the press and other social media. For those who are evaluated through such exercises as England's RAE (research assessment exercise), the pressure to publish in highly ranked journals, to keep one's program going and not simply for promotions, denies time for non-rewarded but publicly useful commitments. In certain cases, departments become little more than appendages to companies and ministries that provide the funding. Elsewhere, public funding is minimal as in the case of England, except for science and technology areas.

This does not bode well for such areas as the humanities and social sciences that are vulnerable to alternative funding sources that can apply brakes to the range and uses of research. The corporation could prevent the results of research from being published because they might appear damning to the company itself or possibly incriminating. The corporation representatives could insert, in the contract for research, the statement that it owns the copyright once the researcher is being paid for the services.

This scenario is not so different from the one described by Henry Giroux with regard to the United States,[6] identified together with South East Asia as among Europe's main competitors in the development of what is being referred to as a process of 'internationalization' – the ability to attract students from outside the EU. These students can pay high fees and, therefore, help raise university revenue. For the bottom line has become a distinguishing feature of universities which, in this age of cutbacks, need to secure the means to survive. The onset of private universities in many countries, including countries such as Turkey, Cyprus, Estonia, Hungary, and other new EU member states, renders the bottom line the key feature of university education provision. The signs all indicate that the university's and other HE institutions' roles in contributing to a democratic public sphere are being severely curtailed. HE institutions continue to take on the roles of 'training agencies' in a system which fails to provide jobs (a jobs crisis), but which promotes the view that the fault lies with people lacking the necessary skills (presenting a 'jobs crisis' as a 'skills crisis').[7]

Areas which do not have an immediate utilitarian purpose suffer, and the relevant departments have to reinvent themselves in 'employability' terms. When the bottom line becomes the key factor, especially in private universities, with many of them benefiting from indirect state funding (e.g. scholarships for students, tax deductions and rebates), then much emphasis is placed on teaching to the test rather than on a balance between teaching and research, unless this research is contract research intended to serve the client's purpose. Furthermore, in a number of countries, such as Turkey, private universities rely on part-time staff. This is also a growing occurrence elsewhere (we read, for instance, of the substantial increase of adjunct faculty in the USA). In Turkey, a situation that can well be repeated elsewhere, they seek to supplement their meager earnings at public universities. In this regard, the co-existence of so called private and public universities is a 'win-win' situation for state and private sector. The state can pay low wages and the private universities need provide no salary at all since they rely on part-time faculty paid at 'piece rate.' This of, course, allows little time for these academics to engage in research. The state is, thus, indirectly supporting the private sector and vice-versa.

And, yet, many Europeans are not accepting this state of affairs. Much of the higher education discourse coming from the

EU and member states is easily perceived by many to be neoliberal in overall tenor. In Central Europe, this has made a mockery of those concepts, albeit elitist and problematic, such as *bildung* (difficult to translate into English, the nearest being 'holistic development of the individual') and the Humboldt conception of the university. If the old university is elitist (a major critique of the Humboldt model with its emphasis on research as the untrammeled pursuit of truth) and not in tune with present-day realities, it requires a transformation which renders it more democratic and expansive in conception. It should not be lean in the same way that the state is said to be 'lean' only in so far as social programs are concerned – as argued at the outset with respect to the huge bailouts of banks in moments of crisis. Criticality, an ingredient of a truly democratic critical citizenship, becomes a casualty in these circumstances.

Students in Austria, Hungary, and other parts of Central Europe have understood this, often joining forces with academics, to mobilize against this state of affairs. The mobilization often becomes international, as with protesting Hungarian students blocking a train of HE experts trying to make it to Vienna for a meeting, as students in both countries coordinated their protest efforts. Proposed reforms of universities in Italy by the deposed right-wing Berlusconi government and communicated by then Education Minister Mariastella Gelmini (one earlier suggestion was that Italian public universities should consider becoming private foundations), led to students occupying the institutions in various parts of the peninsula and islands.

This echoed what happened in Greece on June 8, 2006, when 20,000 students took part in the largest student march for the past two decades, which made its way through downtown Athens. HE becomes a public space for which it is worth fighting. Greece was one of the last countries to resist the reforms being carried out throughout Europe. As a result of resistances to the military dictatorship (1967-1974), Greek HE has been defended by large swathes of Greek society as a public good, a notion enshrined in the Greek constitution, 'according to which Higher Education is provided exclusively by public, fully self-governed and state-funded institutions.'[8] This situation was seriously being jeopardized by the ousted government's (the PASOK Socialist Party-led government of George Papandreou) proposals for reform which also had to be seen in light of the austerity measures being introduced because of the 'debtocracy.' As indicated in a statement, issued by Greek academics and supported by a number of people worldwide, including the undersigned, the previous government (the democratic process was suspended as a technicist government was installed, as in Italy), drastically cut down on public funding for education to the tune of 50 per cent. This was considered amongst the lowest in the EU. The government used the pretext of enhancing 'the 'quality of education' and its 'harmonization' with 'international academic standards.' New hiring of teaching staff was to be carried out at a ratio of 1:10 relative to staff retirement. The bill was passed despite the protests from the Greek and international academic communities. Happily, it was recently repealed as a result of popular pressure, a tremendous fillip for grassroots activism. The Greek academics who flatly refused these proposals stated:

- ... the government proposals seek to bypass the constitutional obligations of the state towards public Universities and abolish their academic character.
- The self-government of Universities will be circumvented, with the current elected governing bodies replaced by appointed 'Councils' who will not be accountable to the academic community.
- The future of Universities located on the periphery, as well as of University departments dedicated to 'non-commercial' scientific fields, looks gloomy.

- Academic staff will no longer be regarded as public functionaries. The existing national pay scale is to be abolished and replaced by individualized, 'productivity' related pay scales, while insecure employment is to become the norm for lower rank employees.
- Higher Education will be transformed into 'training' and, along with research, gradually submitted to market forces.[9]

These type of scenarios, which have been writ large in the 'debtocracy countries' (Spanish academics employed in public universities have taken pay cuts as public employees) provide the context for students and academics to stand out as a social movement that forges alliances with other movements, as was the case in Vienna with kindergarten teachers joining university students and academics (the two ends of the education spectrum) in the 'Unibrennt' (University Burns) actions. Outside Europe, this once again brings to mind the recent protests in Chile.[10]

The coming together of various forces was presumably also the case with the 'debtocracy' protests of the *indignados* where higher education is included among many other issues, such as corruption, unemployment, general impoverishment of several sectors of the population, as a source of indignation. It also provides the contexts for students and academics to stand out as public intellectuals.

One should not underestimate the students' role here. Students have played a significant role in furnishing countries with a stream of public intellectuals as was the case with Carlo Alberto Libanio Cristo (later known as Frei Betto) in Brazil during the military rule (he was imprisoned twice) or Mario Capanna, later a key figure in the Democrazia Proletaria (Proletarian Democracy) Party in Italy, in the Italian student movement of the sixties. The neoliberal reform of universities offers a splendid opportunity for academics and students to continue to join forces as 'public intellectuals' and not only denounce university neoliberal reform, but also turn what is already a public issue (education as a public good) into a broader all-encompassing public concern. This entails that we connect critiques of this reform to the broader critiques of the neoliberal reforms, reforms that have been sweeping across countries and continents, and which have turned society into one large market-place. These reforms and developments often lead to public spaces being turned into commodities, to be bought and sold – spaces that are encroached by corporate forces. And these are the very same forces which have ushered in one of the deepest economic and social crises in the history of humankind.

Academics, students and the population at large need to engage in a struggle for a rethink and renewal of HE as a vital public space within a democracy. Education is important not for simply employability, which, once again, does not necessarily mean employment, but also for the development of a genuinely democratic public environment. The humanities and social sciences need to be defended at all costs; they play a crucial role in this context, despite the famous sound bite from Italy's former Minister for Economic Affairs, Giulio Tremonti, 'La cultura non si mangia' (literal translation 'We do not eat culture.')[11] This struggle must also be complemented by action on the part of social movements and workers' institutions to create alternative forms of provision in these areas. Some of the students protesting in Vienna and other students elsewhere have been exploring paths to pursue. Witness the joint response by two protesting students, one male and one female, from Vienna, in an interview for a book I co-author:[12]

Sit ins/squattings were concentrated in Austrian and German Universities, but there have been some in Italy, Slovenia, Croatia, Serbia, France, the UK ... as well. Social movement? It very much depends on the definition of social movement you want to apply. To us two factors should be present: First of all a plurality of themes/demands that have broader implications for society. And second the involvement of several/different social groups. In Austria we tend to give protests the name 'social movement' quite quickly ... because Austria lacks a long tradition of social movements. Considering our defin-ition, there are certain characteristics of movements to be found in the protest of 2009. By Austrian standards, many people participated. It spread quickly from town to town and even crossing national borders [protesting students in Budapest stopped a train carrying ministers to a meeting in Austria]. There were not just students involved, also university teachers, kindergarten teachers, homeless people and people showing solidarity. But the majority were students. Attempts to work together with unions failed ... so the social basis remained quite homogeneous. The topics addressed by the movement were not reduced to issues of higher education politics. This would indicate a social movement ... The short period of existence of 'unibrennt' is hard to evaluate. In Austria, most of the movements which had existed did have an explosive start, followed by a sudden breakdown. The last movement which could mobilize over some time was the beginning of the green movement, which led to the foundation of the green party in the 80s. The squatting in Austria lasted for a couple of months and was followed by attempts of transnational networking as well as a big conference in March 2009 that again mobilized people. Since then the mobilization declined but still several groups (some of them founded as a result of unibrennt) are politically engaged and active.

The male interviewee went on to shed more light on the educa-tional activities that were organized during the protest activities that attest to the emergence of albeit short-lived capillary forms of power within the context of grassroots democracies, the sort of situation being witnessed in other parts of the world, possibly also in Wall Street at this very moment:

> There was some kind of collective learning/consciousness development ... there have been a lot of activities: Founding of a student self-organized university, a counter-meeting of activists from all over Europe when EU-ministers met in Vienna.... Reading circles, students published several texts and books on topics of the movement and on the movement itself.

The paths indicated lead us to contemplate pursuing several routes. This would include taking back many of the humanities and social sciences, as well as interdisciplinary studies (e.g. cultural studies), to their places of origin – adult education. This should, however, be a struggle on two fronts, the university campus and the community. One should not preclude the other. The community provision outside the university should not serve as an alternative to university provision, except in the way learning settings are created and learning takes place – more dialogical and participative than your conventional HE classroom setting. On the contrary, in this age of draconic cutbacks in these areas, community provision would keep indicating the importance of the humanities and social sciences in the ongoing process of social development. Academics committed to a democratic HE should play their part in this struggle and type of alternative provision, just like scholars such as Raymond Williams and E. P Thompson in Britain, Aldo Capitini in Italy, and countless others have done in the past with their contributions to university extension in the humanities targeting ordinary workers in different parts of their respective countries. It is this provision which would serve as one possible antidote to the current neoliberal discourse concerning university education. And at least one particular project of taking the university back to the people is instructive. It is an initiative of Lincoln University in the UK. It provides a free university education governed by the principles of critical pedagogy, principles that I shall outline and discuss in the very last chapter of this volume.

Among the principles I shall discuss is that of inter-ethnic solidarity in an age when neoliberal politics, buttressing the whole process of the intensification of hegemonic globalization, continues to segregate persons as citizens or non citizens, often on racialized and national lines. I now discuss this issue, with a focus on the region from which I come.

Migration: A Southern European Perspective[1]

Globalization

Globalization is a process which, strictly speaking, has always been a characteristic of the capitalist mode of production characterized by periodical economic reorganization and an ongoing quest for the exploration of new markets. In fact, it is most appropriate to speak, in the present historical conjuncture, of the *intensification* of globalization, brought about through developments in the field of information technology. This process 'not only blurs national boundaries but also shifts solidarities within and outside the national state.'[2] It is a process which finds its ideological articulation in the very same notion of neoliberalism, the critique of which constitutes a thread throughout this book. It is a period in which the notion of mobility seems to be constantly bandied about as if it were a virtue, with total obliviousness to the need, expressed by many, for roots. Mobility is a characteristic of globalization's 'inner' and 'outer' circuits.[3] We can speak of mobility in terms of the threat of the 'flight of capital' in a scenario where the process of production is characterized by dispersal and cybernetic control (outer circuit), and mobility of workers within and beyond the region (inner circuit). Migration is an important feature of the Mediterranean, the region from where I come. As underlined at the 1997 Civil Forum EuroMed:

Immigration represents the emerging aspect, probably the most evident, of the wide process which characterizes more and more the whole planet – globalization. Migrations represent more than a phenomenon, a historical certainty which can be found today, though with different features, in all countries and, in particular, in the most developed (*sic* read: industrially developed). Migration phenomena are becoming more and more important within the Mediterranean basin.[4]

For centuries, according to Ferdinand Braudel, to live in the Mediterranean was to engage in exchange – the *longue durée*. In this day and age, however, the exchange takes on a different form. In terms of mobility of personnel, occurring 'on a scale never seen before in history,'[5] the exchange does not occur on a level playing field. The movement has, for the most part, been unidirectional, a movement from the South of the Mediterranean towards the North. Moreover, as Slavoj Žižek argues, 'in the much-celebrated free circulation opened up by global capitalism, it is "things" (commodities) which circulate freely, while the circulation of "persons" is more and more controlled'[6] The movement has been from North Africa towards Europe and more recently from Sub-Saharan Africa, through North Africa towards Europe. Needless to say, migrants suffer immense hardships in the process, often selling their belongings. Travelling via Libya, they place their life in jeopardy since they are often mistaken for mercenaries (several people still have access to weapons) recruited from Sub-Saharan Africa by the deposed regime to quell and quash the rebellion.

Those who travel – and many have been doing this for years, well before the uprising in Libya – are often placed on rickety boats. It is alleged that they could be forced to swim when danger in the form of advancing patrol boats is sensed or when land is in sight. Drowning occurs frequently. Between July and September 2006, just to provide an idea of the tragedies' scale, no less than 8849 clandestine immigrants landed in Italy. 168 were discovered dead while 144 were dispersed. The Spanish newspaper *El Pais* reported that 490 bodies of immigrants were recovered from the

African and Spanish shores. The same newspaper reports that the *Red Cross* and *Mezzaluna Rossa* believe that the number of clandestine migrants who have disappeared amounts to between 2000 and 3000.[7]

There are many reasons for their departure from their homeland: common reasons would include civil wars fuelled by an arms industry and exacerbation of tribal conflicts, rape and being disowned by family, the attempt among women to avoid female genital mutilation, the negative effects on African farming of subsidies provided to farmers in other continents, the negative effects of climate change, an impoverished environment (the ransacking of Africa) and a colonial ideology which presents the West as the Eldorado and a context for the 'good life,' structural adjustment programs, the quest for better employment opportunities ... and one can go on. But one of the major reasons is that provided by David Bacon with regard to the US and Mexico but which applies globally, namely the quest for low cost labor by corporations and other businesses alike which serves as a 'push and pull factor.' As he argues, hegemonic globalization necessitates migration but it is the same victims of this process who are rendered illegal and criminalized as a result, often victims of the 'carceral state.'[8]

Difference and identity

With regard to immigrants from North Africa and other parts of the Arab world, where unemployment is excessively high and has been the cause of uprisings, it is quite common, in Europe and elsewhere, to refer to immigrants from these areas as simply 'Arab.' They are therefore represented as 'unitary subjects.' The differences in their subjectivities are underwritten – Muslim or Christian,[9] Tunisian, Libyan, Moroccan, Algerian etc. – not to mention also the distinction between Arab and Berber etc. In so doing, we also tend to underwrite the intersections between their ethnicity and other subjectivities (class, gender, ability/disability, etc.).

The situation concerning identity can be quite complex, as indicated by Ahmed Moatassime with respect to the Maghreb where numerous contrasting and contradictory identities cross each other's paths: Berber, Arab and francophone identities.[10] Predrag Matvejevic drew a distinction between identity of being and identity of doing, the latter involving what Carlos Alberto Torres would regard as the opening up of 'areas of negotiation in the context of progressive alliances based on multiple identities and learning communities.'[11]

Unequal Multi-Ethnic Relations: Colonialism Transposed

Against this scenario, we are witnessing the transformation of Mediterranean cities. The population in these cities is increasingly becoming cosmopolitan, in view of the influx of migrants. The global exists alongside the local in a situation of hybridity which has led to what is currently being described as the 'multicultural city'. In certain Southern European cities and towns, the *cupolas* of churches which, for centuries, have been perceived as bulwarks of Christendom against Islam, now co-exist alongside *minarets*. This co-existence of architectural symbols of the different monotheistic religions, that have been the subject of much conflict in the past, is becoming an important feature of the skyline of many a Southern European city. Although one can always argue that they have historically been so in certain Spanish cities where minarets serve as bell towers, *La Girandola* in Seville being the most prominent, and mosques are turned into cathedrals such as *La Mezquita de Córdoba* (now the *Catedral de Nuestra Señora de la Asunción*). On the other hand, the Hagia Sofia or Αγία Σοφία in Istanbul, a secularized museum these days, combines both cultures, while an alternative situation to the Mezquita occurred with the former Santa Sofia Cathedral (now *Selimiye Mosque*) in the Turkish-controlled part of the Cypriot city of Nicosia.

Within this cultural hybridity, a characteristic of several Mediterranean cities, one can easily encounter the tensions which have characterized the region for centuries, exacerbated by the global media in the aftermath of the second 9/11. The phenomenon of multi-ethnicity poses important challenges for education in the Mediterranean as educational policy makers and educators, hopefully aware of the fact that education is not an independent variable (it cannot change things on its own) and should not be romanticized, seek to educate for greater conviviality, a conviviality hopefully predicated on the principle of solidarity rather than on the condescending concept of 'tolerance'.

With respect to Southern Europe, the theme of 'multiculturalism' has been gaining prominence, with conferences and projects on the subject abounding in a number of Latin Arc countries. Much of the discourse is however related to questions of race and ethnicity. During a particular conference on the subject held in Northern Italy in November 1998, no less than sixty Italian educational projects concerning education and multi-ethnicity were presented.[12] Of course, the tensions of centuries of confrontation between cultures cannot be washed away easily.

One must also bear in mind that the relations between ethnic groups are unequal ones, reflecting a non-equitable distribution of resources. It is this which should induce us to avoid a very facile discourse concerning intercultural dialogue or education since, as Handel Kashope Wright argues, this often avoids the fundamental question, a critical pedagogical question: who dialogues with whom and from which position?[13] And this immediately brings to mind a very important feature of the Mediterranean – the scars of Northern colonialism. These scars are felt in many countries of the Mediterranean.

They are often also reflected in those countries, in the North Mediterranean, which are recipients of migrants from southern parts. The idea of post-colonialism, the term used here in a manner which accounts for processes of domination, which have their origin in European colonization, but which extend beyond the period of direct colonization to take on new forms, is something which is relevant not only to the immigrants' country of origin but also to the receiving country. Countries which have been built on migrants, as is the case with Australia, Canada and the USA, rest on a stratification structure which itself can be regarded as colonial. As Peter McLaren has argued, with respect to the North American context, postcolonial pedagogy is '... a pedagogy which challenges the very categories through which the history of the colonized has been written. I am certainly talking about not simply colonial countries, but also about groups who have been colonized in this country.'[14] Colonial relations between countries are transposed to the country of settlement, with certain cultures being regarded as the norm, because of their relation to the dominant group, the Anglo-Celtic group in these countries' case, and others being regarded as subaltern. These are the cultures of those who are regarded as the ethnic 'others.'

Language in a postcolonial context

This situation is not unique to the North American context. With the influx, in Southern Europe, of people coming from the Southern Mediterranean, one can expect to find this reality in a number of countries in the region. A key issue in such a colonial or postcolonial context concerns language. In genuinely multi-ethnic settings, one comes across situations when children receive an education in both the adopted language and the language of origin, a situation which prevailed in the USA and which drew reaction from the ultra right 'English only' movement and more recently the Tea Party. It is a situation which is being undermined by a number of moves and propositions.[15] This has implications also for the teaching of literacy, be it early literacy or adult literacy. Illiteracy is a key feature of education among Southern Mediterranean and Middle Eastern states.[16] John Daniel, former UNESCO Assistant Director General for Education, states unequivocally that 'the Arab region has some of the world's lowest adult literacy rates, with only 62.2% of the region's population of 15 and over able to read and write in 2000-2004, well below the world average of [84%] and the developing countries' average of 76.4%.'

One wonders to what extent lack of literacy also in the mother tongue constitutes a feature of immigrants from these areas and whether bilingualism should constitute a feature of a progressive literacy education in the receiving country. This is a form of cultural hybridity, if you will, which reflects the cultural hybridity which has always been a feature of postcolonial societies (e.g. the learning of Maltese and English in Malta or Arabic and French in Tunisia, with *code switching* between the two languages – colonizer's and colonized – occurring in many contexts). Antonia Darder has written extensively on the need for a bicultural education with regard to people living a bicultural existence, drawing on her own experience as a Puerto-Rican who had to move out of her territory towards California as a result of 'operation bootstrap.'[18] Her writings and advocacy in this regard have greater resonance and apply to not only Hispanics in the USA but also migrants settling in Southern Europe and elsewhere.

Learning to be effectively *bilingual* is part and parcel of a postcolonial education in that it enables one to retain a strong connection with one's ethnic roots, a key feature of one's multiple subjectivities, and at the same time ensures that one learns the dominant language if only not to remain at the periphery of political life. Confronting the colonial by entrenching oneself in the traditional subaltern colonized culture often results in ghettoization. The alternative to this is, of course, assimilation. Assimilation is therefore characterized by a forsaking of one's ethnic roots and one's contribution to the bolstering of a Eurocentric colonial structure of oppression. The ability of people to operate skilfully in their two cultures can be perceived as a source of enrichment of their ethnic culture, in that it does not remain stagnant but proves to be organic, and of the larger society in general.

Decolonizing the Mind?

There is a larger issue with which to contend in such a postcolonial context, one to be faced in both countries that receive migrants and their countries of origin. It is the issue of 'decolonizing the mind,' to use a phrase associated with Frantz Fanon and Ngugi Wa Thong'o.[19] This is one of the great challenges for education in the Mediterranean – providing learning situations which enable participants to decolonize the mind. It should be an education which is based on a problematization of Eurocentric knowledge with its colonizing foundation. It should also be an education which valorizes, without romanticizing, the different cultures of the different groups that form the multi-ethnic society. A critical approach to multi-ethnic and anti-racist education should allow participants to cross their mental and cultural borders, to use a phrase so dear to Henry Giroux.[20] Crossing borders would, in this context, entail that one begins to understand something about the culture of others, religion included. Needless to say, a critical multi-ethnic education, as part of a larger multicultural education predicated on the valorization of difference and identity, involves a process of democratization of the entire educational system in terms of curricula, texts and the entire pedagogical process. The curriculum is a selection from the cultures of society. It would be pertinent to ask: In whose interest is the selection being made? Whose cultural arbitrary, to use Pierre Bourdieu's term, is reflected in the curriculum? These questions would be posed in any society in terms of the social differences involved – gender,

class, race, ethnicity, sexual orientation, ability, religious affiliation etc. These questions will be posed with greater vehemence
the more socially differentiated and *secular* a society becomes.

There are those who would argue, in this context, for a 'multi-
centric' education, one which allows the traditionally marginalized not simply to be 'included' or 'grafted' onto 'the existing
order' but, to echo bell hooks, to 'move from the margins to the
centre.'[21] The traditionally marginalized ethnic groups must
become major actors in the curriculum and not simply adjuncts
to a cast formed of people from the dominant ethnic groups. In
contexts such as these, the Freirean approach to pedagogy would
strike me as being relevant. It is based on the valorization of
subaltern cultures, conceived of not solely in terms of class and
ethnicity but also in broader terms to incorporate gender,
sexuality, race and other forms of identity. These subaltern
cultures serve, according to the Freirean conception, as the point
of departure for a genuinely democratic pedagogical process. An
education intended to 'de-colonize the mind' should also be
characterized by coherence in that it views critically those events
which provide the basis of European colonization. I refer in
particular here to events surrounding Christopher Columbus
(Cristobal Colon in Spanish) and his voyage to America, often
celebrated uncritically in this part of the world (certainly in 1992,
although there have been some laudable exceptions, especially
among fringe groups in Spain). And this, despite the fact that it
can be regarded as a voyage that gave rise to 500 years of
genocide, the main victims being the indigenous peoples of the
Americas.

The issue of 'decolonizing the mind,' however, entails more
than this and is a process which lies at the heart of what I regard
as being one of the main challenges facing several Mediterranean
countries, particularly those in the region's North which are
recipients of immigrants from the South. It is the challenge of
providing a critical and genuine anti-racist education.

As far as the issue of cultural contestation is concerned, one must, of course, recognize the complexity of the region in this context. At the risk of reproducing a 'colonial' argument, I would submit that, for all their subtle and not-so-subtle forms of discrimination (often institutionalized forms of discrimination), there are countries in the Mediterranean, particularly those around its Northern shores, which offer greater 'spaces' than others in this regard. It is more likely that one discovers greater opportunities for the affirmation of different cultures in settings which are characterized by a spirit of secularization than in settings wherein, for instance, a particular religious culture is hegemonic (e.g. Catholicism in Malta, Islam in a number of Arab countries and elsewhere, the Greek Orthodox religion in Greece). There are cases where it can be argued that the presence of a secular state does not signify a spirit of secularization in the country or certain regions. Turkey strikes me as a case in point with respect to the last mentioned.

In non-secularized contexts, there are severe limits to the degree of multicultural democracy, as conceived of in this chapter, which can occur. Not that discrimination, in the form of racism, homophobia and sexism, is a feature of only non-secularized contexts; it exists everywhere. It is common knowledge, however, that certain countries of the Mediterranean lag behind others regarding the acquisition, by traditionally marginalized groups, of what would generally be regarded, in other countries of the region and elsewhere, as 'taken for granted' rights. The Arab uprisings of the past year can be regarded as, apart from a quest for a greater share of the economic pie (see Chapter 10), a struggle for the affirmation and achievement of such rights and civil liberties. Many people have placed their bodies on the line in these countries, giving up their 'today' so that the rest of the country hopefully live a better 'tomorrow' characterized by some of the liberties enjoyed in Western contexts, even though there are also those fighting battles with an unmistakably religious purpose, and possibly a fundamentalist religious purpose, in mind. The writings of such intellectuals as Nawal El Saadawi and Magda Adly, both from Egypt, and contributors to the periodical, *Mediterraneo. Un Mare di Donne* ('Mediterranean Review: A Sea of Women'), stress the issue of human rights and civil liberties with respect to the situation of women.[22]

Politics of Representation

The various situations of conflict which characterize this region, and which can cause tension in multi-ethnic societies, render comparative studies in different areas, including comparative religions, very pertinent. Studies such as these which can take different forms, depending on the level, can help foster greater understanding. Many of the Southern European regions of the Mediterranean have traditionally been steeped in the Christian religion, mainly Catholic and also Greek Orthodox. It is imperative, in a truly multi-ethnic environment, that knowledge of the different religions is provided in schools and in other educational sites. One ought to mention, here, projects such as the one promoted by IRRSAE in Puglia, Southern Italy, which focuses on the curriculum with special reference to the three great monotheistic religions of the Mediterranean.[23] There is always the danger, however, of providing a caricature. The complexity of the situations can easily be ignored, with religions being represented in simplistic terms and possibly distorted.

The representation of different religions should therefore be approached with the utmost seriousness and best preparation possible, with special emphasis being placed on the teacher or media worker doing justice to the different religions involved. Misconceptions regarding Islam abound in the Western world. Countries in Southern Europe, which are recipients of immigrants from Arab countries, are no exception. One of the greatest misconceptions regarding Islam is its strong identification, in the minds of many, with the Arab world. In effect, the Arab world is characterized by difference also in terms of religious denomination, while Islam is a truly international religion. Islam knows no geographical, racial and ethnic boundaries. For instance, this religious affiliation is prevalent among the many Somalis who cross the Mediterranean and settle in Southern European countries.

It is common to find distortions of religions in many school texts, as Mahmoud Elsheikh so clearly points out with regard to the way Islam is presented in Italian manuals. Some of the distortions are as serious as that of attributing the words of the Qu'ran to Mohammed rather than to God (the Koran as the object of revelation) and of producing representations, in miniature, of the Prophet when it should be common knowledge that representations of Mohammed and God are not allowed by the Qu'ran.[24]

With regard to societies in the northern part of the Mediterranean, a postcolonial education would entail a critical engagement with a cultural heritage that reflects a colonial past, as in centres of colonial power such as Spain and Portugal, and a past marked by crusades against the Ottoman Empire. The focus here would be on the politics of representation that underlies this heritage. Exotic and often demonic representations of 'alterity' abound throughout this cultural heritage, be it the colonized indigenous populations of the Americas or the 'Saracen', the latter constituting the traditional 'Other' in relation to whom 'Christian Europe' was constructed.

We often barely recognize that the silver and gold that adorn much of the relics in our churches and palaces were extracted at the expense of human lives, the extermination of indigenous lives and those of others, in Latin America and elsewhere. Human tragedy, in the form of genocide and rapacious colonial greed, lies behind the veneer of those 'things' judged as resplendent, 'things of beauty' perceived as a 'joy forever.'[25] And all this is based on the tragedy that results from *otherising*, positioning those who are different as 'other.' The 'other' becomes the subject of a particular kind of construction, a form of *Orientalism* in Edward Said's sense of the term. It is a demonization reminiscent of the French imperial construction of the Algerian and other colonial subjects, based on a false scientism, exposed by Frantz Fanon in *The Wretched of the Earth*.[26]

Even authors of canonical works in the receiving country are guilty in this regard and have been severely criticized by Mahmoud Elsheikh on these grounds. Exponents of Italian humanism, including one of its major figures, Petrarch, denigrated the Arab culture, considering it as ushering in a barbarian period which was responsible for the adulteration of the ideal of Greco-Roman antiquity. Dante Alighieri is not spared any of these criticisms, especially for the manner in which Mohammed is portrayed in the *Divina Commedia*, with the great Florentine poet guilty of reproducing distortions generated by popular accounts in the West. And this despite the fact that Dante, like other medieval European poets, owes much to Islam in the development of his work, a point registered by Spanish scholars such as Miguel Asin Palacios, while scholars such as Angel Gonzales Palencia highlighted Arab contributions to cuisine and other aspects of life.[27]

Indeed much of the celebrated domains of study and the institutions which promoted them owe a lot to the Arab and, one should add, Iranian cultures, be it literature (and here one can also include pre-Islamic poetry), science, mathematics, medicine and philosophy. The same applies to those hallowed centres of learning that are the universities; the oldest of those that are extant is to be found in an Arab context. As far as Islam goes, Lê Thánh Khôi indicates how the oldest universities in Europe have been influenced by this religion, and states that the teaching of medicine at Salerno was supported by the school of *Kairuan* while the University of Bologna and others adopted certain forms of Muslim teaching , such as the art of argumentation and the dialectic, and the *ijaza*, the 'authorization to teach' (or 'license to teach').[28]

The Mediterranean which contributed to the formation of Europe is not just the Greco-Roman Mediterranean but a much larger region which includes its North African shores. There was a time when the demarcation between North and South was blurred or non existence, certainly during the time of the Golden age of Islamic culture, the age of Ibn'Rushd (Averroes), with Córdoba being the centre. The contribution did not simply consist of the Arab world, and more specifically the world of Islam, serving, for centuries, as the 'Other.' It consists also of substantial contributions to many important areas, as outlined above. Referring to what he calls the 'debtor's syndrome', Elsheikh states forcefully:

> ... the person to whom one is indebted is constantly a hated person; particularly if the creditor, as in this case, is a strange body, rejected by the collective consciousness, hated by the political, social, cultural and religious institutions. If anything, the rage against the creditor, in these circumstances, becomes an almost moral duty and a necessary condition for the survival of that society.[29]

A similar politics of representation characterizes the realm of popular culture in the Southern European – or Northern Mediterranean – region, with the Sicilian marionette shows, involving Crusaders and the Predator (often the Saracen 'Other'), being a case in point. In introducing immigrants to popular culture, one ought to be wary of its contradictions. It often contains elements which constitute a denigration of aspects of the immigrants' own culture.

The concerns in this chapter are intended as signposts for postcolonial approaches to education in the Mediterranean, predicated on the concepts of equity, social justice and multicentricity. They focus on what to avoid. In the final chapter I will make some recommendations, writing from an educationist's perspective, bearing these and other concerns, raised in the earlier chapters, in mind. They are intended to provide a look to the future. However I will now proceed with further considerations of Muslim and Arab youth with regard to their construction (including misrepresentations) post 9/11 and also the role they play in confronting neoliberalism and its discontents in what has, albeit romantically, been called 'the Arab Spring.' In my view, we should speak of a groundswell which we must continue to follow closely as events continue to unfold. Hopes are frequently frustrated, though they spring eternal. And there seems to be 'no going back' on the insurgents' part.

9

Facets and Representations of Muslim Youth[1]

I have recently been a frequent visitor to Istanbul where I even had the pleasure of teaching summer school at Bogazici University. On my penultimate visit to Taksim and the surrounding area, en route to the Galata Tower, the city's vibrant din was enhanced by the sounds emanating from one of those 'tourist trains' we are now accustomed to finding in many places. The only difference was that this train featured not tourists but an accomplished blues band belting out some classics in a manner that would have made greats such as Robert Johnson, Bessie Smith, Muddy Waters and B.B. King proud. This was not an imported band. It was fully composed of young Turks (no pun intended). And of course, I have no indication of the religious beliefs, if any, of the band members. The scene however captured much of the spirit that prevails in this city where West meets East and South meets North; where Kemalists (followers of the modernist secularism of Mustapha Kemal Atatürk) co-exist with extreme Marxist oriented left wingers; where Ottoman, European and North American cultures blend in a variety of ways; where a strong Muslim culture makes its presence felt alongside other religious cultures in the context of a secular state. This, for me, is Istanbul. And Pierre Hecker's account, in an edited volume on Muslim and Arab Youth,[2] of heavy metal in Turkey gestures in this direction. Would this be representative of many other contexts inhabited by Muslim youth? This would be difficult to tell given the heterogeneity of Muslim contexts. In this chapter, I shall comment on this volume – *Being Young and Muslim: New Cultural Politics in the Global South and North* – edited by Linda Herrera and Asef Bayat, which brings together different discussions on several aspects of Muslim and Arab youth (not to be conflated) in different international contexts. It goes to show how Islam knows no international boundaries and the volume serves to indicate the complexities surrounding Muslim and Arab identities which we should bear in mind lest we lapse into the kind of simplistic and essentialist discourse that has abounded for quite some time, and more so since September 11 2001 and other attacks, deemed, in several quarters, as a reaction to a globalizing neoliberal world. I would say upfront that the volume does justice to the heterogeneity of these contexts ranging from Western contexts such as Germany, the Netherlands and France to Arab contexts such as Egypt and Morocco, to the sub-Saharan African context of the Gambia, to the Middle East, to Indonesia, to Iran.

What this book certainly manages to do successfully, in my view, is capture a sense of the complexity of identity formation among Muslim youth as they navigate the contours between different cultures and lifeworlds, including those perceived as modern or postmodern, once again highlighting the dangers of stereotyping and cultural essentializing. Muslim youths move, interact, appropriate, reject, and transform. It is this sense which comes across throughout the book. That blues band in Istanbul could well have been composed of Muslims. That would not have surprised me in the least, given the insights I subsequently gleaned from this volume.

The book however challenges the stereotypes about Muslim youth. It does so at a time when youth in general, as many have been arguing, and Muslim youth in particular, have been on the receiving end of a media onslaught. Henry Giroux has been writing, persuasively, of a war against youth and children (3). Images of 'degenerate' youth have been constructed by a variety of adverts worldwide. Youth have been maimed or exterminated by senseless wars especially the war in Iraq. Muslim youth have been projected as terrorists, suicide bombers and having no way out save through their engagement in militancy. And the blame for this has often been placed on radical Islam and other similar forms of fundamentalist orientations. This book does not deny the appalling conditions in which several youth, Muslim or otherwise, find themselves in the global South. Indeed we are informed, in the introduction by the editors that 90 per cent of world's young are concentrated in a global South characterized by upheavals and significant – extreme in certain cases – levels of poverty. We are told that economic exclusion, corruption, under-employment and deprivation among vast segments of youth render the transition to adulthood problematic. But then the various chapters indicate the complexity concerning the identity formation of such youth in the circumstances. Indeed, in the Western-backed Indonesia, under the ruthless regime of Suharto, modernization and capitalism, left in the hands of multinationals and conglomerates to the total exclusion of the marginalized popular classes, have led certain youth to resort to fundamen-talist approaches to Islam. Salafi youth, marginalized by the lack of a popular economy, sought gratification in fighting jihad wars abroad, specifically defending Moluccan Muslims against attacks by Moluccan Christians.

Others however react to similar situations differently. For instance, in one of the most revealing pieces, consisting of an exposition and analysis of narratives involving two youths, Karim and Dina in Egypt, we come across the level-headedness of a desolate youth whose family became déclassé and for whom the future in Egypt looked bleak. The narratives are indicative of how these youth adapt to situations, including those of machismo encountered by Dina, and eschew some of the more radical pathways made available to them. Karim would have no truck with terrorists and with the killing of innocent people. Not only that, but he comes across as being quite perceptive in his analysis of issues concerning the Middle East and the world in general, although solace is found in the Qu'ran or else in hashish.

Others react to overconsumption patterns in particular ways. Engaging in radical political activity in such an autocratic context as Saudi Arabia is a non-starter. But youth seek ways and means of rebelling against the system, creating their own heroes in the process. The more impoverished youth engage in stealing cars and in the kind of hair-raising, life threatening sport that would have made Hemingway proud.

The *tahfit* is the classic example here. Ostensibly coming across as youth madness, manifestations of which can be attributed to other sports and activities in other parts of the world, this is an attempt at challenging law and order, and family order at that, and could therefore be easily regarded as political, given the nature of its subversion.

Perhaps the most fascinating aspect of strategies devised by Muslim youth is their engagement with aspects of a globalizing culture, notably hip-hop and rap, as well as heavy metal, and cyberspace. In contexts governed by a dominant belief system, as is often the case in the global South, the indulgence of youth in heavy metal sends shockwaves among the older generation who are often quick to denounce this as a manifestation of Satanism. This however applies to both North and South. In this respect, we see how the situation concerning Turkish youngsters embracing this form of globalized music is quite in keeping with trends all over the world. However it remains to be seen what sort of resistance is being offered and what is being targeted in these specific contexts. Surely the legacy of Mustapha Kemal (Atatürk), and therefore the state politics of secularism in Turkey, is bound to help foment these situations.

In the case of cyberspace, we come across an interesting account of how Palestinian youth resist the imposition of an occupying force which limits their participation in a range of educational and other activities. They resist this imposition through a variety of means, not least cyber-resistance. As the old English adage goes, in this context, 'necessity becomes the mother of invention' and it is in these circumstances that youth are at their most inventive and at their most ... enterprising (for want of a better and less commercial word). There cannot be power without resistance, although that resistance is never external to the power structure itself, in this case hegemonic globalization and the internet. Resistance emerges in music. Blues was for years the cathartic cry of the oppressed Afro-American on the plantations of North America. It subsequently found its place among other subaltern voices in different parts of the world, for example in subaltern Naples (see the music of Pino Daniele, as an example). It has been complemented by other forms of black affirmative music such as reggae, calypso and more recently hip-hop and rap, the signifiers of which suggest deep political meanings. Street children in Brazil have turned to rap to inveigh against the system just as boys and girls 'n'd hood' have been doing in the USA. We now hear of the mass media in Britain, especially the tabloids with their penchant for gross sensationalism, demonizing any kind of rap denouncing the ills carried out against the Arab world and against Muslims, all in the wake of 9/11/2001 and 7/7/2005. 'Jihad rap' is the demonizing term used. And yet Red Swedenberg's systematic analysis, in this volume, of Fun^Da^Mental's music indicates that the press is ever so ready to draw a caricature of such politicized music providing the sort of reductionist interpretation that adds to the fabric of Orientalism. Swedenberg shows how this music is multifaceted and certainly postcolonial in the broadest sense of the term, posing questions rather than providing prescriptive responses. And the range of situations scoured is broad enough to extend well beyond the Muslim or Arab or Persian worlds. This analysis is, in my view, a clear example of cultural studies at its political best. It is concerned not only with text and textuality and floating signifiers but primarily with political content and the problem posing of concepts, situations, and classifications as popularized by the media.

While there is more to this music than simply resistance, this aspect cannot be ignored in a context where a merciless purge of Muslim youth takes place, tarring all with the same brush. This is a manifestation of the culture of fear generated in the aftermath of 9/11/2001 in the USA and especially 7/7/2005 in London, not to mention 4/11/2004 in Madrid. Quite fascinating is the account by Mustafa Bayoumi of retrenchment and resistance by Muslim youth in the USA after September 11 2001 and their demonization and racialization by members of the public, journalists and the authorities alike, being viewed as the 'potential terrorist' within: 'They think we are all Bin Ladens' as the Syrian mother of an engineer in the USA once put it to me in a conversation. And now this is one aspect and reality of identity formation that Muslims in the USA have to come to terms with as they attempt to survive and prosper in their home. And of course, the same applies to Muslim youth in other contexts in Europe. In contrast, Bin Laden is a cult hero among 'USA bashing' hip-hop followers in Niger, as indicated in Adeline Masquelier's account in the same volume.

It would have been impossible in a volume such as this to avoid discussions concerning the construction of citizenship and identity formation in a place like France given the entire controversy surrounding the *hijab*. Two papers in this volume tackle this subject, one by Schirin Amir-Moazami contrasting the situation of Muslim youth in Germany and France. The situation in the former country, which still has its problems, is considered much better, as far as identity formation of Muslim youth is concerned, than that obtaining in Sarkozy's France.

I cannot but agree with the whole discussion raised by Moazami regarding the fallacy of persisting with the concept of 'tolerance' in this day and age, symptomatic as it is of a system of social relations governed by unequal power relations. Tolerance is, in my book, too condescending a term. It is for this reason that I have often shown my perplexity with regard to

Freire's usage of the term in his pedagogical writings and the usage of people close to him who have even published a volume of his writings under the title of *Pedagogia da Tolerancia*! Tolerance should, in my view, have little room in a situation of dialogue, or authentic dialogue, among cultures that seek to redress the unequal power relations concerning different ethnic groups within Western society. It is for this reason that I consider Moazami's discussion around tolerance, drawing on Wendy Smith, most important in a volume such as this and in relation to a context such as Europe which exalts 'intercultural education', often treated uncritically without any proper understanding of its underlying unequal power dynamics. The word 'tolerance' if anything underscores the existence of such unequal power relations.

And yet we see from this chapter and the very well crafted one by Palestinian scholar André Elias Mazawi how the politics of *laïcité* in France is used in an attempt to fashion a different kind of Muslim, a sort of 'European Muslim.' Mazawi indicates how the school becomes an important space for the struggle over the citizenship and identity of these students who are forced to reposition themselves to maintain their politics of difference, in light of impositions deriving from the overall politics of what seems to be a fossilized notion of *laïcité*. It is part and parcel of the struggle for hegemony over the meaning of the public sphere, in this case the contemporary French or European public sphere. In my view, a secular state, the hallmark of the modern state, is one which valorizes social difference and which safeguards the right of every person to express his or her individuality in a manner that does not impinge on the individuality of others. Wearing a *hijab*, a crucifix or the Star of David is an individual act; this is different from placing a crucifix, Star of David or Muslim symbol in a public space.

Arab Groundswell, Digital Youth and Challenges of Education and Work[1] – with Linda Herrera

The revolutionary spirit in Tunisia, Egypt and Libya was stirring in virtual communities before it spilled out to a wider spectrum of society. In each country the trigger for revolution and determination to confront the status quo and replace the leadership, was the wrenching story of a fellow citizen. In Tunisia, 26-year-old Mohammed Bouazizi, dubbed 'the father of Arab revolution,'[2] set himself on fire on the sidewalk in front of the local municipal building where he sought, but never received, justice. Bouazizi, who worked in the informal economy as a fruit and vegetable vendor since he was a teen, was continuously harassed, fined, and beaten by police officers including a female officer. One day he simply could not take it any longer and, like Czech hero, Jan Palach in 1968, perpetrated self-immolation. In Egypt Khaled Said, a 28-year-old from Alexandria was dragged out of a cyber café by two police officers and brutally beaten to death in view of witnesses. The 'Call for the Revolution of January 25' which brought down the presidency of Hosni Mubarak originated from the Arabic Facebook page 'We are all Khaled Said' that was founded as an anti-torture youth movement in the martyr's honor. The call for the revolution, printed on the backdrop of a half-Tunisian and half-Egyptian flag, read '25 January 2011 Egyptians Uprising Against Torture, Corruption, Poverty & Unemployment'.

In Libya the street protests, which eventually led to a bloody civil war involving NATO bombings and around 40,000 casualties, began in Benghazi on 15 February with the news of the arrest of human rights lawyer Fethi Terbil. In all cases the tipping point for what would become a mass broad-based revolution was the circulation of a compelling story of the humiliation, abuse, and flagrant flouting of rights of a fellow citizen. But in the background, especially in Egypt and Tunisia, rising food prices, high rates of youth unemployment, and the escalation of the most abusive kinds of crony capitalism were just as important. In other words, issues of civic injustice may have triggered the street protests, and no doubt state violence against protesters fuelled them, but economic injustice and insecurity have always been looming as sources of mass discontent.

In an interview with the Maltese English language daily *The Times*, Abd El Aziz Hegazy, former Egyptian Prime Minister and a key figure in the bid to create a new Egypt, chairing Egypt's National Dialogue, states that the Egyptian revolution concerned three things: freedom, the empowerment of the poor and unemployment. 'When the revolutionaries first came, they shouted "Bread!" Then they called for social justice, democracy and freedom. The revolution,' Dr Hegazy insists, 'is as much economic as it is political.'[3]

Egypt and Tunisia share a set of socio-economic and political features that made each of them ripe for revolt. The populace faces the range of vulnerabilities that come from the dismantling of the welfare state, accelerated privatization, crony capitalism, and corruption that drains national resources and skews distribution. In both countries the young are part of a youth bulge, meaning that roughly two thirds of the population are under thirty years of age. They suffer from exceedingly high rates of unemployment, which hover at around 25 per cent in Egypt and 31 per cent in Tunisia. Unemployment rates are highest among educated youth with high school and university diplomas, and even higher for females. Among youth who find employment, the overwhelming majority of them labor in insecure, very precarious circumstances with no fixed contract, benefits, and unlivable salaries. Their inability to secure a livelihood prolongs their dependence on parents, their ability to marry and form families, and also pushes them, especially males, into second and third jobs. And in both Egypt and Tunisia the digitally savvy youths have been ahead of the global curve in how they use new media for campaigns, organizing, and a range of politically subversive activities.

Cyber Politics

Cyber activists and scores of 'ordinary' users of social media and the internet have acted as a generational collectivity and society's conscience. They have taken an uncompromising stand against injustice, corruption and abuse of power.[4] Aided by tools of new media and digital communication tools, youth cultures throughout Egypt, Tunisia, Libya, Syria, Bahrain, Yemen, Jordan, Morocco, Algeria, Iran, are indicative of a democratic ethos, of people power sweeping the region. Digital youth have effectively used new media for a range of political action,[5] from coordinating strikes, election monitoring, exposing corruption in 'naming and shaming' blogging, and building anti-torture campaigns. This internet generation has a very firm grip on rights, civic liberties and democratic accountability and has well honed the art of single issue campaigns using new media. For the most part youth movements using new media platforms exhibit greater adeptness at articulating a way forward for civic and political rights, and are on more shaky footing when it comes to economic rights, fair labor practices, and distributive justice.

To be sure, one of the most high profile campaigns born on the social media platform of Facebook was the April 6 youth movement. It came onto the scene in 2008 to support the strike of industrial workers in the town of El-Mahalla El-Kubra. This student activist group quickly became the most active and visible group with a leftist orientation and has consistently used new media in innovative ways to effectively build activist coalitions nationally and internationally. It has also consistently supported workers' movements and formed alliances with them during the revolution. To be sure, there has been a strong labor presence in Egypt's revolutionary movement. Workers converged on Tahrir Square and other places throughout the country to clamor for better pay and working conditions; the largest union called for a general strike. Just after the fall of Mubarak in February 2011 around 4000 workers from the Assiut (Upper Egypt) cement company staged a sit-in to demand permanent contracts, a profit-sharing system and an end to the daily-wage system of remuneration for work. On February 25, labor leaders in Egypt established the 'Coalition of the 25 January Revolution Workers.' But it remains to be seen how the military will respond to a mobilized and organized force and if youth will join workers in larger numbers.

The two groups, laborers and educated youth, have potentially much to gain in forging a stronger coalition on labor issues and workers rights. High school and college graduates have a great deal in common with their less educated laboring counterparts when it comes to the insecurities of the job market and degradation of labor rights in a period of late neoliberalism. This is symptomatic of an ever-expanding bifurcated working class comprising those with high levels of education who have become déclassé and those with little or no formally acquired skills whatsoever – a characteristic of societies elsewhere, including Europe, but writ large in the Southern Mediterranean.

Economic Justice?

Most of the countries in the region undergoing upheaval are characterized by huge disparities in wealth and unemployment. Issues concerning economic engagement and distribution are at the heart of the struggles involved in most cases, certainly in Tunisia and Egypt. It remains to be seen whether the democratic changes that are being promised will be deep rooted or simply serve as a cosmetic exercise with other members of the ruling oligarchy simply replacing the man (the rulers have invariably been men) at the helm. There were protests in Tunisia in this regard, before the country went to the polls, and the November 2011 parliamentary elections in Egypt took place as the second phase of the revolution, with violent standoffs between protesters and security forces. But as one protester on Tahrir Square stated in an electronic exchange with one of us, the clamor is for 'an end to the influence of the former regime, through proper prosecution and punishment of all members of the former regime. The prosecution and punishment of everyone who has been involved in the killing of innocent protesters. Clear actions from the current government and SCAF towards proper change in the country.'[6]

Pressure is being brought to bear on the military caretaker government in Egypt not only so that it does not renege on its promise of a smooth transition to civilian rule, but to ensure a much more democratically equitable economic system. The call is also for an economy that incorporates large amounts of youth in meaningful employment and which provides greater and meaningful educational expansion at all levels. This economy must be complemented by a greater democratic politics of redistribution that is believed to be capable of addressing the country's deep rooted social and economic inequalities. One also wonders whether this is a digitally mediated revolution intended to allow a greater middle class sector, extending beyond the present oligarchy, to gain a greater share of the cake. In short, is a country like Egypt having its version of a bourgeois revolution?

In a conversation with Antonio Dall'Olio, the Director of *Pax Christi International* (Italy), a Cairo Professor referred to the fact that the Islamic world lacked a 'French revolution' as well as a Vatican Council II which ushered in a process of renewal in the Western world.[7] Is the former occurring right now in specific Arab contexts such as the Egyptian one? To what extent would this larger bourgeoisie connect with the aspirations of a burgeoning social sector including that expanding precariously-living working class that incorporates people with skills and qualifications which were formerly the staple of the middle class, albeit perhaps the petit bourgeoisie?

These economic and social considerations, however, raise further questions: How is digital technology enabling youths to acquire skills for greater participation in a broader and more meaningful labor market? And more to the point, will this generation use their skills for political mobilization and revolutionary change to work in the service of work and redistributive justice? So while these revolutions pose questions regarding the use of the digitally mediated technology for revolutionary purposes and how digital networking can lead to street and cross-border mobilization, they also raise issues about what the economic future holds in the transition and post-transition contexts. The economic factor is not to be underplayed in these situations given the marginalization of the many for the lavish benefits of the few; for the most part, the traditionally Western-backed oligarchy (certainly in Egypt and Tunisia). Members of the ruling families have, alas, pandered successfully to the whims of even progressive Western organizations such as the International Council for Adult Education which made Susanne Mubarak Honorary President for 1994-1998, as period issues of its otherwise very progressive and social justice-oriented journal *Convergence* indicated!

What alternative economic policies are necessary to accommodate these skills? What alternative proposals are being put forward for a different economic approach that counters the situation of mass unemployment among youth in the area? What role does digital technology play in this regard? Is the increase in use of digital technology contributing to a further brain drain among youth? On the contrary, would a greater democratic liberalization of the country lead to a re-draining of digitally savvy

Arab youth who can now work from the comfort of their home in Egypt? They would thus eschew the kind of post-9/11 anti-Arab and anti-Muslim sentiments prevailing in the countries to which they emigrated. Could the democratization of Arab states lead to more digitally mediated cross-border economic ventures involving youths of different Arab countries? We would add that these economic ventures can complement the political digitally mediated ones which, it has been argued, albeit romantically, can give rise to a pan-Arab youth movement. The jury is still out as to whether the protesters constitute a movement, something which applies not just to Egypt and the rest of the Arab world but also the protest movements in Europe, the USA and beyond where the Occupy movements have become part of the protest landscape. In an exchange carried out electronically on 8 July 2011, the protestor at Tahrir Square stated:

What is currently happening in Egypt is not clear. I cannot call it a movement yet. What happened in January [2011] was a whole country saying 'That's Enough.' Overthrowing the government and the president was a decision we all agreed on. Once that was done, people are not sure how to move and in what direction. In that sense, we are faced with groups of people trying to take advantage of this new freedom by trying to stir people in a certain direction, those are the Muslim Brotherhood, or the salafis, or the SCAF. We can see people taking advantage of the lack of trust in the police forces, and the lack of police forces to begin with, they do so by breaking traffic laws, by attacking the police, by bombing churches and using weapons. We see the former regime trying to create chaos among the protestors, by sneaking thugs in the middle of the protests to start riots and fights, and make people lose trust in the revolution and in the protestors. Finally, we see the majority of the population struck by all this chaos surrounding them, confused by how the values of the 18 days of the revolution have disappeared completely and have been replaced with violence and hatred. A lot of people are trying to get organized into groups and decide on the direction in which to go, but for the most part the majority of the population is frustrated to find that what happened several months ago was as though it never did. People now are divided in how they feel towards this revolution, many are too afraid of the future and of the chaos taking place now, that they feel we should stop all this nonsense. People are good at judging the actions of others and not taking any action themselves.[8]

Finally, how does one bridge digital inequality with these economic considerations in mind? Answers to these questions can only emerge gradually as events in this long struggle for democratic and economic renewal in the Arab world continue to unfold, alas at a huge cost in terms of human lives in a number of cases, especially the Libyan (a carnage) and the Syrian ones. It still remains to be seen whether the revolutions will be brought to the political conclusion augured by those who took to the streets and shed their blood in the process. As if this is not worrying enough, one wonders what the future holds beyond the change in power structure in terms of addressing important economic issues and ending the cycle of poverty in which many people in the region find themselves (although this was not the case with Libya which among other things offered free education and free health care, as well as grants to newly-wed couples). This is where some of the most formally educated and experienced persons, many of whom appeared in the media abroad, will need to step up to the plate. And Libya provides excellent examples with the person selected as interim prime minister and his rival, both established academics abroad with ground-breaking research to their credit.

It is also imperative that foreign imperialist interests be kept in check, which sounds 'wishful thinking' in the case of Libya with the involvement of NATO and key figures such as Hilary Clinton, David Cameron and, 'first out of the blocks,' Nicolas Sarkozy. The country's oil resources lead to all sorts of conspiracy theories, backed by the fact that similar interventions have not been contemplated elsewhere, also with regard to equally despotic regimes in countries which are main oil suppliers to the USA and other Western powers.[9] The situations differ from country to country, as well as the resources available. Tunisia has organized political parties which were outlawed by the ousted leader. Others need time to get the representative democratic act together, characterized by 'redistributive justice.'

Striking the balance between different tribal and societal interests is crucial in certain contexts both for democratic and economic renewal. Striking a balance between democratic and economic reconstruction will also be key further down the road. Ousting from power, as a result of mass unemployment and economic marginalization, was ultimately that which crooked a beckoning finger to the autocratic leaders in Egypt and Tunisia.

One issue is crucial. Will legacies of free public education and healthcare, as was the case in Libya, be maintained and taken up in other countries? Or will the revolutions, which claimed countless lives, pave the way for the tyranny of the market, as has been the case with Eastern Europe following the collapse of the Berlin Wall or in stateless nations such as that of the Palestinians? Protesters and the new governing political class, as well as trade unions and other social organizations, would do well to learn from the protests of the *indignados* and those occupying the streets in various cities in North America and Europe, in ensuring that education and labor market training, as well as healthcare, are safeguarded or developed as public goods and not be allowed to degenerate into consumption goods.

11

Education and the MDGs[1]

A pre-CHOGM[2] plenary seminar, jointly organized by the Commonwealth Consortium for Education and the University of Malta's Faculty of Education in the Autumn of 2005, as part of the Commonwealth's People's Forum, made me engage in some critical reflections on the implementation of the United Nations' Millennium Development Goals (MDGs) in Education.

It would be worth recalling that the eight MDGs are:

- eradicating extreme poverty and hunger,
- achieving universal primary education,
- promoting gender equality and empowering women,
- reducing child mortality,
- improving maternal health,
- combating HIV and malaria diseases,
- ensuring environmental sustainability,
- developing a global partnership for development.

The eight Millennium Goals have been accepted by most nations. They have often been decried for being too vague and hardly ambitious. Others have argued that they do not tackle the root causes of much of what is wrong with a world that has been characterized, and alas continues to be characterized, by an unequal distribution of resources and by a colonial legacy that makes itself present in a variety of forms not least through what is termed 'globalization from above.' 'Globalization from above,' as I had occasion to remark earlier on, is used with reference to the dominant form of globalization; it refers to policies and processes that advance the interest of the economically more developed countries, and trans-national corporations, and promotes the view that market forces should take precedence over policies that advocate the needs of people, especially the poor.

It is very unlikely that any of these Millennium Development Goals will be accomplished satisfactorily by the target date of 2015 or even much later if we persist with the kind of economic policies that continue to place profit before people. For these challenges to start being confronted seriously certain drastic actions need to be taken.

Unless the institutions which support 'globalization from above,' namely the World Trade Organization, the World Bank and the International Monetary Fund, are brought to their senses and are prevented from persisting with their support for neoliberal policies that continue to sap Africa, the Caribbean and other victims of European colonial power of their life, through the so-called Structural Adjustment Programmes (SAPs), we will not have effective and well funded educational programmes that promote greater social justice, that spread greater knowledge concerning health and environmental issues and contribute to the development of effective means of distributing resources internally.

Only through policies which help us conceive of education as a public and not a consumer good can one start to effectively educate with the achievement of these and alternative goals in mind. Only through the signing and close observations, by every government, including that of the world's only superpower, of accords such as the Kyoto Protocol will educational programmes for 'greater environmental sustainability' gain greater meaning. And such treaties need to be rendered accessible and widely disseminated. They cannot remain couched in a language understood only by experts, mainly scientists and economists.

Only through policies that shackle the arms industry that exploits tribal and ethnic conflicts through its sale of conventional weapons and supports autocratic regimes, can we go some way towards tackling some of the proposed and alternative goals. This should be part of a process that makes countries stricken by poverty and by unequal resource distribution spend more on educational programmes and less on repressive measures including incarceration and the buying of weapons.

Only through a global process of education worldwide that enables us to engage with history and economics critically, to understand the processes involved that have led to an unequal global distribution of resources, and a broad-based non-Eurocentric humanistic education, can we seek to combat such current malaises as widespread racism and xenophobia on the one hand and unscrupulous 'racist' employment policies on the other. These types of education will hopefully take us some way towards a 'global partnership for development' – a genuine programme of education for solidarity across regional, national and international, including North-South, borders.

An investment in educational programmes in areas and regions of the world that are marked by extreme poverty should be complemented by investment policies that will provide a better match between skills and jobs in the same areas and regions. This would help prevent a further 'brain drain' resulting from what is effectively a process of 'education for export,' the process that has characterized colonial and neo-colonial policies to date. In this regard, economic power blocs such as the EU and the US need to revise their 'fortress' economic and agrarian policies for the way they impinge negatively on economic development in Africa and elsewhere. With a daily billion-dollar subsidy provided by the wealthy countries to their farmers, people from poor countries that depend on agriculture will find it hard to feed and educate their children.

We need to avoid an approach to education that exalts only one type of knowledge, invariably knowledge derived from the Western and Northern Hemispheres, as 'official and legitimate knowledge' and marginalizes knowledge deriving from south of the equator areas, including indigenous knowledge and educational traditions. The marginalization and denigration of knowledge from the South is one of the legacies of colonialism that still has to be confronted adequately since it perpetuates a culture whereby people and agencies from this region of the world are represented in terms of a 'deficit' model. It is the sort of model that portrays them as people who should be held wholly responsible for their plight. Besides, individuals and institutions that are now finding some of this knowledge profitable should not be allowed to privately patent it, without providing compensation to the people who have been developing this knowledge over the years.

Related to this is the consideration that Western models of development, including those that entail gender mainstreaming (one ought to remark that development models are not gender neutral), do not necessarily work in some of the contexts that are hardest hit by poverty. There needs to be recognition of and support for agencies (including NGOs), from the area, committed to addressing such issues as women's issues, AIDS/HIV, environmental issues, agrarian economic development, etc. These agencies are more likely, than their Western counterparts, to have an intimate knowledge of the cultural contexts in question. They and other international organizations and movements, including many situated in the west, play a major role in monitoring compliance of governments regarding the MDGs and advocating for more and better aid (in the early seventies, the wealthiest nations had committed themselves to 0.7 per cent of their GDP to be reserved for international aid), 'justice in trade' (fair trade) and debt write-off as key to the attainment of the proposed and alternative goals. In so doing, organizations such as these engage, through a series of local/global linkages, in what is referred to as 'globalization from below.' This consists of an international networking of groups and social movements that engage in acts of resistance against and offer alternatives to the dominant form of globalization referred to earlier, one which, to echo the Portuguese sociologist and legal expert, Boaventura de Sousa Santos,[3] marginalizes a number of people and regions through the unequal exchange it produces.

12

Conclusion: A Critical Approach to Education

Introduction

This chapter continues in the same vein as the previous ones in which signposts for an alternative approach to education and cultural work have been provided, not least in the penultimate chapter (Chapter 11) dealing with the Millennium Development Goals which though difficult to realize by the established deadline remain important points of reference when critiquing current policies in a variety of aspects of life, especially health and education. In this final chapter, I draw on what is commonly referred to, in educational parlance, as critical pedagogy, which draws inspiration from Freire and a host of other writers and movements. While the people involved demonstrate a variety of approaches, one common element is that they underscore the political basis of education. Education is not a neutral enterprise and heuristically can be regarded as serving either to 'domesticate' and strengthen the status quo and therefore keep in place much of the ills, economic, social and environmental, addressed in the preceding chapters, or else 'liberate' in the sense of contributing to the ushering in of a new world in which principles of social justice and ecological sustainability are held uppermost. We associate this thinking with the work of Paulo Freire, though he is not the only one who thought, wrote and worked along these lines. One major exponent of critical pedagogy, Peter McLaren defines critical pedagogy as 'fundamentally concerned with the centrality of politics and power in our understanding of' education and learning.[1]

Market Ideology

This approach, as part of a more critical approach to education, strikes me as serving as an antidote to much of the neoliberal policy discourse that has dominated thinking over the last thirty years or so and which has been the object of critique in all the chapters in this volume. We have been swamped by policies and formulations about education strongly connected with the market ideology, referred to, throughout the volume and by several others, as neoliberal. Education is seen as a consumption rather than a public good with responsibility for learning being placed on the individual. The Chilean experience discussed in Chapter 2 represents the most extreme form of this approach where even state education is conceived of, or was conceived of, this way by the perpetrators of a most bloody dictatorship. It remains to be seen whether the changes augured by those struggling for more jobs and greater democratic spaces in the Arab world will represent a departure from this kind of approach which was prevalent in places like Egypt during the Mubarak period, even though jobs for the majority of Arab youth and other people were 'thin on the ground.'

The Integral State and Education

In this regard, one cannot separate discussions concerning education from discussions concerning the state, the discussion that introduced this book (Chapter 1). There has been a whole debate concerning the role of education and the state. Roger Dale analyses the immensely complex relationships occurring between capitalism, state, and education. Drawing on Claus Offe, he analyses the process whereby education is linked to both capitalism's legitimation function, by persuading us that inequality is not endemic to the system but a consequence of our different 'abilities,' and to the production of necessary 'human capital' for national and global economic ends. Dale argues that the ways those tensions are felt and addressed through education are central to our understanding and experience of the world. In this regard, reference should be made once again to Peter Thomas' recent highlighting of Gramsci's notion of the 'integral state.'[2] This entails a comprehensive view of the state's role in the consolidation and the provision of a context for the consolidation or contestation of hegemonic relations. The separation of political and civil society, the latter used by Gramsci in a manner that differs from the way it is used today as a third sector between the state and industry (see Chapter 1), is done specifically for heuristic purposes. The state embodies both, as Thomas underlines. Equally heuristic, in my view, is the separation between the ideological and repressive as the two cannot be entirely separated unless in terms of degree. Institutions have both their repressive and ideological sides and this applies to the health sector, religion, education and other areas.

Hegemony

Hegemony, explained earlier on in this volume, is the means whereby social forces, manifest throughout not only civil society but also what is conceived of as political society (again the division is heuristic), are, as Thomas notes, transformed into political power within the context of different class projects. I would also add to this conceptualization the view, mentioned by Thomas and certainly by Gramsci, following Marx, that the integral state has a strong relational dimension. For instance, critical educators write about the need for new democratic kinds of social relations in production (inspired by Gramsci here), the public sphere (see for instance the Participatory Budget experiments in Porto Alegre and elsewhere), education and other aspects of social and economic life. These 'prefigure,' to use a verb adopted by the late Paula Allman, a new form of state, through its more democratized horizontal social relations of production. This prevents us from reifying the state as a 'thing', from engaging in 'thingification' as Phil Corrigan would put it. It is also manifest in Gramsci's conceptualization of every relationship of hegemony being a pedagogical relationship.

The importance of this theorization for those who believe in a politically engaged education, for the gradual ushering in of a different world, cannot be missed. It is perhaps for this reason that Gramsci has had such a considerable influence on critical pedagogy, as the works of authors such as Paula Allman, Jean Anyon, Michael Apple, Antonia Darder, Henry Giroux, Deb J Hill, Margaret Ledwith and David W. Livingstone so clearly indicate. What emerges from Thomas's careful exposition is the notion, emphasized by Gramsci, that different historical formations are at different levels in terms of their development of civil society. These formations differ in the quality of the relationship between state and civil society. This applies to East and West, and, pertinently given the discussion in Chapter 8, North and South. As Thomas rightly notes, there are social formations in the West, including the most Western of the West,[3] which are bereft of many institutions of civil society.

Hegemony and Education

The hegemonic apparatuses need to be built and consolidated to become the channels of the ruling class's lifeworld (*lebenswelt*). The implications for educational activity are enormous. Education is viewed in the broadest sense, the way Gramsci viewed it, seeing it as central and integral to the workings of hegemony itself, and the way many critical pedagogues view it. Notable here is Henry Giroux, very much inspired by Gramsci, who developed the notion of 'public pedagogy.' Education plays an important role as a hegemonic apparatus.[4] This insight should allows us to view theories and philosophies in terms of their being institutionally embedded, serving as a hegemonic apparatus and being integrated in and therefore being ideologically over-determined by the integral state. Educators, seeking to highlight the politics of education, can draw on this insight. They can engage in uncovering ways by which dominant educational philosophies serve as hegemonic apparatuses for the 'integral state.'

Hegemony and Lifelong Learning

In these times, for instance, this concept would enable educators to expose the dominant philosophies of lifelong learning closely connected with the hegemonic notions of 'responsibilization' and 'employability' as linked to the neoliberal integrated state and its relations with, for instance, the supranational state that is the EU. Many of the claims made in relation to the fallacy of lifelong learning, distorted with respect to its original concept as 'lifelong education' as propounded by UNESCO, would seem hollow. There is an over emphasis on work, employability and ICT. All this indicates that the discourse thus far is removed from a broad conception of education that takes on board the different multiple subjectivities characterizing individuals. It still gravitates around the notion of a knowledge economy which, as certain research from Canada shows, is not the reality people are made to believe it is.[5] It might not lead to the level of employment and financial rewards being anticipated given the global competition for the few high paying middle class jobs available.[6]

This discourse also limits human beings to two-dimensional persons, consumers and producers, rather than expands the conception to embrace a more holistic view of persons who have the skills to engage critically and collectively not only *in* but also *with* the work process and also engage in the public sphere, that domain of democratic practice which critical pedagogues such as Giroux, perhaps inspired by Dewey and Habermas, have been writing about for years. This would entail a notion of citizenship that can be called 'really and critical active citizenship,' embracing the 'collective' (in the sense of people working and acting together, complementing each other), rather than the notion of the atomized individual citizen that is often promoted by the dominant discourses surrounding citizenship. I am here referring to the idea of atomized individuals who facilitate *governmentality*, in Foucault's sense of the term. Governmentality refers to the state's production of citizen behavior according to its policies, fostering mindsets and practices that allow subjects to be governed 'at a distance.'[7] Many of the issues being faced throughout society call for coordinated collective actions involving both ICT and the streets and squares, as the numerous demonstrations in Greece and other parts of Europe, as well as many parts of the Arab world, have shown (see Chapter 10) albeit not necessarily attaining the desired outcomes (the struggle remains an ongoing one, as I have emphasized time and time again). They are also public, and not simply individual, issues that entail social responsibilities.

As the literature on this kind of action has shown, such an ongoing social engagement entails constant learning and relearning, pointing to a notion of lifelong learning that, as expounded on by a number of writers from a critical perspective,[8] constitutes a refreshing alternative to the one that prevails in the dominant discourse. It is a type of lifelong learning that has been occurring for years but which has not always been recognized as such. It is one which is inextricably intertwined with ongoing popular struggles for the creation, safeguarding and enhancing of democratic spaces in which men and women live as social actors. This is all part of the process of renegotiating the apparatus of hegemony.

Solidarity

Furthermore, we require a critical pedagogical approach to education that takes as its point of departure a new and more pressing notion of solidarity, one which cuts across class, gender and racial lines. This brings me back to the point made in Chapter 5. It should be an education or kind of political activity that focuses squarely on not different identities in total isolation from each other in a process of segmentation but on the totalizing structural force of capital, the 'universe of capital' if you will. This is what the thousands who have been taking to the streets in various cities of Europe and the USA as well as beyond seem to be gesturing towards and I use 'gesturing' since we need to adopt a tentative and groping approach to our analysis of events here. Yes there was racism, sexism and many other -isms before the inception of capitalism but here we have a totalizing structuring force that is predicated on segmentation on social class, gender and racial lines. At the heart of this approach, there should be an anti-racist education which does not sanitize the unequal and violent, physical and symbolic relations that exist and are promoted by an ever globalizing and criminalizing capitalist system. On the contrary it should be one that induces human solidarity, avoiding misplaced alliances. It would seek, through problem posing, to unveil the fact that both the so-called and often self-styled autochthonous working class and the immigrants share a common fate: that of being oppressed and subaltern. Both are victims of a ruthless process of capitalist exploitation.

Higher Education

One other point concerns higher education. This area is under vicious attack by those taking advantage of structures which require renovation and perhaps a wider purpose in society. As indicated in Chapter 6, rather than being widened to render the university and institutions of higher education more responsive to the democratic needs of society, the discourse is being reduced to one regarding another form of business governed by the principles of the market. And yet one would expect these institutions to serve much wider causes than those of the economy and employment. They can well provide, and happily some indeed do provide, against all odds, responses to some interesting innovations, in different pockets throughout society, with respect to different forms of production. These entail different and more horizontal relations of producing, as well as the identification of alternatives to what is being produced. Instead, as shown, these institutions are exposed to a discourse that is divisive in its encouragement of diversification in terms of research, teaching and regionally responsive universities, with ramifications for the Ancient Greek notion of praxis (reflection upon action for improved action, involving the codification of such reflection into theory). There is the danger that teaching is to be separated from research. And praxis is a central concept in critical pedagogy based on the old Socratic maxim, reproduced by Plato in the *Apologia*, that an unexamined life is a life not worth living. Quite laudable in this regard are initiatives such as that at Lincoln University (mentioned in Chapter 6) that revive in some way the old notion of independent working class education, a kind of university education rendered gratis to the popular classes with certification endorsed internationally by a number of academics, even if dismissed by the relevant state apparatuses. This alternative university education is based on the principles of critical pedagogy where knowledge is shared not for instrumental reasons (i.e. for work) but for the social end of helping in the formation of politically engaged social actors.

In light of some of the points made in the preceding chapters and in the burgeoning critical pedagogical literature, one hopes that the scope of knowledge focused upon, as a result of epistemological curiosity, is broad enough to incorporate insights derived from South and North, East and West. It would be a body of knowledge that foregrounds subaltern views, including the best from feminisms, critical racism theory, working class education, indigenous knowledge, environmental studies and social movements' learning (including subaltern social movements' learning). This would constitute the grist for a critically engaged insurrectional pedagogy.

A Critical Approach to Education in 'These Times.'

I conclude by providing a brief and selective overview of some important breakthroughs in critical education, without any claim to being exhaustive.[8] Many of the concepts regarding public pedagogy and the role of intellectuals as transformative intellectuals and public intellectuals have been dealt with by Henry Giroux in a number of works. Giroux is a founding figure in the field. He actually broadened the notion of education[9] to include several sites of public pedagogy ranging from schools to cinemas and youth entertainment areas, as well as the consumer culture and military culture ideologies. He does this when analyzing the devastating effects and 'terror' of neoliberal policies and when arguing for universities, schools and other learning agencies to serve as democratic public spheres.

Michael Apple, for his part, argued for the democratization of the curriculum which he presents as a site of contestation mirroring other sites of struggle such as the state and the domain of textbook publishing. He has been detailing the economic, political, and ideological processes that enable specific groups' knowledge to become 'official'[10] while other groups' knowledge is 'popular.' Over the past two decades, he has critically examined the social movements that internationally exercise leadership in educational reform. He has also analyzed progressive reforms that can provide models for critically democratic alternatives. Antonia Darder, cited extensively in this volume and a co-author of one of the chapters, has engaged with issues of cultural democracy and consistently with notions of culture and power concerning conditions of schooling in disenfranchised and racialized communities,[11] work which, as I indicated earlier on, is most relevant to some of the issues raised in Chapter 8.

Marxist thinking has had a great impact on critical pedagogy. Paula Allman is one educational writer who did much to engage directly with Marx's own writing. Issues here concern ideology and the production of consciousness, dialectical thinking, education's role within the 'base-superstructure' relation, and education's role in the reproduction of the social conditions which enable the ruling class to retain and consolidate power.[12] One person who certainly 'Marxified' critical pedagogy is Peter McLaren especially in his work from the late nineties onward. And one must recall the earlier work on adult learning and a socialist pedagogy by the Botswana-based educator, Frank Youngman.

The critique of capitalist education and more recently neoliberal education has come from various quarters. Feminist writings have served to expose the contribution that education makes to the consolidation of patriarchy as well as its potential to confront it both within and outside formal institutional settings. This includes work by Dorothy E Smith, Gail Kelly, Kathleen Lynch, Mary O'Brien, the Taking Liberties Collective group, Becky Francis, Sara Delamont, Luisa Muraro, Angela Miles, Jane Thompson, Valerie Walkerdine, Arlene McLaren, Sandra Harding, Kathleen Rockhill, Mary Belenky and Jean Barr.

Sara Delamont, for instance, has argued that both sexes are diminished by institutional sexism in all sections of the education system so that the lack of women in engineering is no more serious than the lack of men training as infant teachers or nurses.[13] Jane Thompson has applied the ideas and convictions of modern feminism to the curriculum and practice of women's education and adult education. She is concerned not simply with access issues but with politicizing the significance of women's lived experiences and with developing theories to explain the changing conditions of women in global capitalism. She has exemplified the linking of women's activism to both educational change and wider social and political movements concerned with fighting inequalities. Similarly, Kathleen Lynch contributed to feminist thinking in education through her work on the intersectionality of injustice. She has examined ways by which gendered problems of recognition are interwoven with issues of re/distribution and representation. She has also highlighted the importance of relationality and emotions for understanding the dynamics of injustice in education and has developed the concept of 'affective' equality to explain how carelessness is a key equality problem for society and for educators. Angela Miles' main theoretical contribution is the concept of 'integrative feminisms' and 'multi-centered' (as opposed to de-centered) social movements.[14] She draws on Adrienne Rich's integrative feminist perspective on education that recognizes the specificity of women's history, interests and value. The focus here is on women being able to recognize and name the world themselves very differently from the way men have done – rather than simply having equal access to male education.

Of particular importance here is the work of Mary Belenky et al.[15] They focused on how women learn and what is distinctive about their learning, drawing their insights from responses to questions posed to 135 female interviewees. In Italy, the pedagogy of Anna Maria Piussi (with Luisa Muraro and Adriana Caballero, she belongs to the University of Verona and the *Diotima* group of women philosophers) refutes the paradigm of victimization and feminine discrimination. The key idea is to value, also through education, women's difference and differences in general and to help gain awareness of oneself and discover one's voice as woman engaged in relationships with others.

bell hooks, referred to in Chapter 8, brings an Afro-American perspective into the debate on women and education. hooks foregrounds the issue of race and ethnicity in this context. A whole body of work, not least that found in the journal, *Race, Ethnicity and Education*, addresses such concerns. Among the major sources is W.E.B. Dubois who wrote extensively on the empowerment of black students and an education which enables them to see themselves through their own eyes rather than through the white perspectives provided by traditional education.[16]

More recently, we come across the writings of George Sefa Dei who formulates an integrative anti-racism education – race, class, gender, sexuality and disability interactions through a race-centric lens[17] – and examines black youth disengagement from school as a 'push out' problem. He also develops the concept of Africentric schooling as a counter-vision to conventional white-centric education, and promotes anti-colonial thinking in education, underscoring the importance of indigenous knowledge. Closely related to this area is thought associated with postcolonial and decolonizing studies in education. I have argued, in Chapter 8, that, as a site of struggle, education has constituted a key vehicle for the 'colonization of the mind.'[18]

There is a body of literature on education connected with the disability movement. It eschews the medical/deficit model and adopts the social constructivist approach. Writing around this field, often directed at policy making, but not only, can be found in such outlets as the journal *Disability & Society*. Some writers such as Susan Peters in the USA have drawn on Freire to explore empowering pedagogical insights in this context. The literature exposes forms of disabling environments and education and explores possibilities for an enabling education for all. In this view, the barriers are regarded as disabling, difference is valued and the strengths of individuals are emphasized. Contributors like Mike Oliver[19] shift the emphasis from individual deficits to disabling environments when turning around a series of conventional 'deficit' questions regarding what is awry with the relationship between the individual and the environment.

The theme of inclusion is not simply confined to social relations. It extends to human-earth relations, often in the context of 'ecopedagogy.' This is a holistic approach to pedagogy that conceives of people as primarily relational beings acting in communion not only with human others but with all other creative beings within the cosmos. The work of Edmund O'Sullivan (b. 1938), drawing on Thomas Berry, is instructive here.[20]

The foregoing should be sufficient to indicate the range of work from which insights can be gleaned for an approach to education governed by concerns with increasing social justice. The language, areas of enquiry and type of education advocated are a far cry from that of standardization, entrepreneurship, league tables, monolingual learning and technical-rationality that we find in the dominant discourse on education and public policy. Despite the all pervasiveness of a discourse on education which is imperialist and smacks of hegemonic globalization, there are many persons who work against the grain, providing postcolonial and social justice oriented disruptions and which see education as one area which can contribute to the transformation of the world. It would be a transformation from the one in which we live into one which is more genuinely democratic and ecologically sustainable in which people and the rest of the environment are placed before profit. In the words of Raymond Williams, they proffer 'resources of hope.'[21]

Notes

Chapter 1

1. An earlier version of this chapter appeared as an opinion column, 'The State, Public Pedagogy and Learning' in *Truthout* 8 October, 2010.

2. Paulo Freire, in Nita Freire as interviewed in Borg and Mayo, 2007, *Public Intellectuals, Radical Democracy and Social Movements. A Book of Interviews*, (New York: Peter Lang) p. 3.

3. See Corrigan, P., Ramsay, H. and Sayer, D. (1980), 'The state as a relation of production,' in Corrigan, P. (ed.), *Capitalism, State Formation and Marxist Theory*, (London: Quartet Books).

4. See Zygmunt Bauman on this in Macedo, D. and Gounari, P. (2006), *The Globalization of Racism*, (Boulder, Co: Paradigm).

5. See Douglas Kellner (2005) *'Media Spectacle and the Crisis of Democracy: Terrorism, War, and Election Battles,'* (Boulder Co: Paradigm).

6. Ibid.

7. See Henry A. Giroux 'Brutalizing Kids: Painful Lessons in the Pedagogy of School Violence,' in *Truthout* 8/10/2009.

8. The major theorist here is Antonio Gramsci. See Gramsci, A. (1971). *'Selections from the prison notebooks,'* (Q. Hoare & G. Nowell-Smith, eds. & trans.) (New York: International Publishers).

9. Definition culled from Canadian sociologist David Livingstone's 1976 paper, 'On hegemony in corporate capitalist states: Material structures, ideological forms, class consciousness, and hegemonic acts,' published in *Sociological Inquiry*, 46, 235-250.

10. See Raymond Williams, 'Base and Superstructure in Marxist Cultural Theory' in the 1976 Open University Press Reader, edited by Roger Dale, Geoff Esland and Madeleine Macdonald (now Arnot). *'Schooling and Capitalism. A*

Sociological Reader,' (Milton Keynes: Open University Press). The piece originally appeared in New Left Review (1973) and it later appeard in Marxism and Literature.

11. I am using the term here as used by Gramsci in whose work the apparent separation between civil and political society is done simply for heuristic purposes. The concept is well expounded by Peter D Thomas (2011) in *The Gramscian Moment. Philosophy, Hegemony and Marxism*, Chicago, IL: Haymarket Books.

12. See David Held's 2006 version of his classic, *'Models of Democracy,'* (Cambridge and Malden MA: Polity Press), p. 172.

Chapter 2

1. An earlier version appeared as an opinion column, 'From Chile to the Twin Towers. Two September 11ths' in *Counterpunch* Weekend Edition September 16-18, 2011

2. See Noam Chomsky (2011), *9-11: Was There an Alternative?(with a new essay written after the assassination of Osama Bin laden)*, New York: Open Media Books

3. See Peter Mayo (2011) 'From Chile to the Twin Towers. Two September 11s' in *Counterpunch*, Weekend Edition Sept. 16-18, http://www.counterpunch.org/2011/09/16/two-september-11ths/. See also Ariel Dorfman (2011), 'Epitaph for another September 11' in *The Nation*, 19th September, http://www.thenation.com/article/163056/epitaph-another-september-11

4. See Charlotte Baltodano, C (2009) 'A Freirean Analysis of the Process of Conscientization in the Argentinean Madres Movement' in Abdi, A and Kapoor, D (eds.) *Global Perspectives on Adult Education*, New York and Basingstoke: Palgrave Macmillan.

5. See Henry A Giroux (2005), *Against the New Authoritarianism. Politics after Abu Ghraib*, Winnipeg: Arbeiter Ring Publishing.

6. See Polin So (2011) 'The Fight to Make Education a Guaranteed Right: Chilean Students vs. the Nation's President,' in *Truthout*, 29th August, http://www.truth-out.org/fight-make-education-guaranteed-right-chilean-students-vs-nations-president/1314638583.

Chapter 3

1. Previously published as a jointly authored opinion column 'Reflections on the Blockade, a Tricontinental Vision, and the Capacity to Share. The Promise of Cuba' in *Counterpunch*, Weekend Edition October 7-9, 2011. It developed as a jointly authored series editors' Preface to Anne Hickling-Hudson, Jorge Corona Gonzalez and Rosemary Preston (eds.) (2012) *The Capacity to Share: A Study of Cuba's International Cooperation in Educational Development*, New York and Basingstoke: Palgrave Macmillan.
2. See Robert C. Young (2003) *Postcolonialism. A Very Short Introduction*, Oxford & New York: Oxford University Press.
3. See George Galloway (2006), *Fidel Castro Handbook*, London & New York: MQ Publications Ltd, p. 206.
4. Young, op. cit, p. 17.
5. See Saskia Sassen's interview in the Italian left wing daily, *Il Manifesto*, 17th August 2011 with the title: 'Con i riots la storia volta pagina' ('History turns a new leaf with the riots'). The reference here is to the recent riots in England but connections are also made with other protests in Europe, notably Madrid and Greece. Sassen sees historical analogies with the transition from modernity.
6. Anne Hickling-Hudson, Jorge Corona Gonzalez and Rosemary Preston (eds.) (2012) *The Capacity to Share: A Study of Cuba's International Cooperation in Educational Development*,New York and Basingstoke: Palgrave Macmillan.
7. Humberto Marquez (2005). Venezuela declares itself illit-

eracy-free. *Inter Press Service News Agency.* 28th October, 2005. http://www.ipsnews.net/africa/interna.asp?idnews= 30823 Retrieved October 2, 2011.

8. Mike Cole, (2011). *Racism and education in the UK and the US: Towards a socialist alternative.* New York & London: Palgrave Macmillan.

9. See http://www.ecosherpa.com/news/cuba-only-country-with-sustainable-development/ We are indebted to Professor Paul J Pace from the University of Malta for making this source and the one that follows known to us.

10. John Bachtell: 'Cuba shows that planet Earth can be saved with the help from environmentally sustainable socialism' in *greenblog 09/03/09,* http://www.green-blog.org/2009/09/03 /cuba-shows-that-planet-earth-can-be-saved-with-the-help-from-environmentally-sustainable-socialism/

Chapter 4

1. Previously published as an opinion column 'Nicaragua's Pedagogical Effort 30 Years on' in *Truthout,* Saturday 30 October 2010

2. Zuniga, M. (1993), 'Popular Education and Social Transformation in Nicaragua' (Zuniga interviewed by Peter Mayo) in *Education* (Malta), Vol. 5, No. 1., pp.33-40. 3. Interview with Zuniga in Carmel Borg and Peter Mayo (2007), *Public Intellectuals, Radical Democracy and Social Movements. A Book of Interviews,* New York: Peter Lang.

4. Zuniga (1993) op.cit.

5. For a comprehensive appraisal of the literacy and popular education campaigns in Nicaragua and the rest of the country's educational system, see Robert Arnove's 1986, *Education and Revolution in Nicaragua,* New York: Praeger, and its sequel *Education as Contested Terrain Nicaragua (1979-1993),* Boulder: Westview Press.

6. Zuniga (1993) op.cit.

7. For an extensive account of education in these contexts see the chapter by Carlos Torres and Daniel Schugurensky in Carlos Alberto Torres' 1990 book, *The Politics of Nonformal Education in Latin America,* New York: Praeger.

8. Information provided by former coordinator of the Grenada Literacy Campaign, Didacus Jules – electronic communication.

9. I would recommend the work of John Hammond here. See for instance his 1991 interview 'Popular Education in the Midst of Guerrilla War: An Interview with Julio Portillo' in *Journal of Education* (Boston) , Vol. 173, No. 1, pp. 91 - 106.

10. See Myles Horton and Paulo Freire's 1990 'talking book,' *We make the road by walking, Conversations on Education and Social Change,* Philadelphia: Temple University Press.

11. See Paco Ignacio Taibo II's biography of Che Guevara: Senza Perdere la Tenerezza. Vita e morte di Ernesto Che Guevara, EST, 2000 – Italian version of *Ernesto Guevara También conocido como El Che.*

12. Interview with Maria Zuniga in Carmel Borg and Peter Mayo (2007), *Public Intellectuals, Radical Democracy and Social Movements. A Book of Interviews,* New York: Peter Lang.

13. Ibid.

Chapter 5

1. Earlier draft appeared as Peter Mayo (2011), 'The Meaning of May Day Celebrations' in *Truthout,* Thursday, 05 May 2011

2. Giroux, H.A (2010) *Hearts of Darkness. Torturing Children in the War on* Terror, Boulder, Colorado: Paradigm Publishers.

3. Butler, J (2009) *Frames of War. When is Life Grievable?*, London: Verso

4. Bauman, Z (2006), 'The crisis of the human waste disposal industry.' In Macedo, D & Gounari, P (Eds.)*The globalization of racism.* Boulder, Colorado: Paradigm Publishers.

5. This is adapted from the concluding section of Mayo, P

(2007) 'Gramsci, The Southern Question and the Mediterranean' in the *Mediterranean Journal of Educational Studies*, Vol. 1, No. 2, pp. 1-17.

6. See Antonia Darder (2011a) *A Dissident Voice, Essays on Culture, Pedagogy and Power*, New York and Frankfurt: Peter Lang, and (2011b), *Culture and Power in the Classroom.* 20th anniversary edition, Boulder Colorado: Paradigm.

7. See Nawal El – Saadawi (1997), *The Nawal El Saadawi Reader*, p. , London and New York: Zed Books.

8. The final paragraph is adapted from my essay on Antonia Darder in Peter Mayo (2012), *Echoes from Freire for a Critically Engaged Pedagogy*, New York and London: Continuum (in press)

Chapter 6

1. Previous version appeared as a news analysis 'Politics of Indignation: As Rome Burns' in *Truthout*, Wednesday, 23 November 2011.

2. See S. Mclean (2011) 'Pride of Place' (pp. 42-44) in *RSA Journal*, Autumn issue, p. 43.

3. I am indebted to participant Loris Viviani for this information.

4. I am indebted to participant Patrizia Morgante for this information.

5. See D. Kapoor, (2009) 'Globalization, dispossession and subaltern social movements (SSM). Learning in the South,' in A. Abdi & D. Kapoor (Eds.), *'Global perspectives on adult education'* (pp.71-92). London & New York: Palgrave Macmillan. p.71.

Chapter 7

1. An earlier version appeared as an opinion column, 'Universities Burn: A View From Europe' in *Truthout*, Thursday, 27 October 2011.

2. See 'Higher Education Under Attack: An Interview With Henry A. Giroux,' C. Cryn Johannsen; 'Margins of Everyday Life,' *Truthout*; 'Beyond the Swindle of the Corporate University: Higher Education in the Service of Democracy,' Henry A. Giroux, *Truthout*; 'The Fight to Make Education a Guaranteed Right: Chilean Students vs. the Nation's President,' Po Lin So, *Truthout*; 'What I Wish Jill Biden Would Talk About With Respect to America's Community Colleges,' Keith Kroll, *Truthout*.

3. Interview with student protester against neoliberal reforms of the university in Vienna, carried out electronically, August 2011.

4. See former EU Commissioner for Education, Jan Figel: Figel, J. (2006). The modernization agenda for European universities. Public talk on the occasion of the 22nd Anniversary of the Open University of the Netherlands. See also CEC. (2006a). Communication from the Commission to the Council of the European Parliament. Delivering on the Modernisation Agenda for Universities. Education, Research, Innovation. Brussels: European Commission on Education and Communication.

5. See Philip G. Cerny (2007), 'Paradoxes of the Competition State: The Dynamics of Political Globalization, in *Government and Opposition*,' Volume 32, Issue 2, pages 251-274. The term is also used by Bob Jessop: Jessop, B. (2002), '*The Future of the Capitalist State*,' Oxford: Polity Press. It was used in relation to educational policy by Stephen J Ball: Ball, S.J. (2007). *Education plc private sector participation in public sector education*. London: Routledge.

6. See Henry Giroux and Susan Searls Giroux (2004), *Take Back Higher Education* (Routledge), and Henry Giroux (2007), *The University in Chains. Confronting the Military-Industrial-Academic Complex*, (Paradigm) as examples of his many writings in the area.

7. Judith Marshall: Marshall, J (1997) 'Globalisation from Below. The Trade Union Connections' in S. Walters (Ed.) *Globalisation, Adult Education & Training. Impact and Issues*, London: Zed Books; Leicester: NIACE.

8. Initiative of Greek academics I am indebted to Prof. Maria Nikolakaki, University of Peloponnese, Greece, for this source.

9. Initiative of Greek academics.

10. See PoLin So, 'The Fight to Make Education a Guaranteed Right: Chilean Students vs. the Nation's President,' in *Truthout*. Retrieved on 14/10/2011.

11. Moni Ovadia, 'Ministri senza vergogna (Unashamed Ministers)', in *L'Unità*, 27 November 2010.

12. Leona English and Peter Mayo (2012), *Learning with Adults. A Critical Pedagogical Introduction*, Rotterdam and Taipei: Sense.

Chapter 8

1. This chapter draws selectively from two previous works to which new insights are added: Peter Mayo (2001) 'Globalization, Postcolonialism and Identity: The Role of Education in the Mediterranean Region' in Nada Svob Dokic (ed.), *Redefining Cultural Identities: The Multicultural Contexts of the Central European and Mediterranean Regions*, Zagreb, Institute for International Relations; Peter Mayo (2004 hb; 2008 pb) *Liberating Praxis.Paulo Freire's legacy for Radical Education and Politics*, Westport: Praeger (hb), Rotterdan and Taipei: Sense (pb). Authorization to draw on and republish material from Chapter 5 of this book is provided by ABC-Clio.

2. Carlos Alberto Torres (1998), *Democracy, Education, and Multiculturalism. Dilemmas of Citizenship in a Global World*, Maryland, Rowman and Littlefield. p. 71.

3. Ibid. p. 92

4. Laboratorio Mediterraneo (1997), *Obiettivi e Mezzi per il Partenariato Euromediterraneo. Il forum civile euromed*, Napoli, Magma, p. 551

5 El Saadawi (1997), *The Nawal El Saadawi Reader*, London and New York, Zed Books, p. 122.

6. Slavoj Žižek (2004), *Iraq – The Borrowed Kettle*, London: Verso, p. 34.

7. Source: ANSA, Madrid 28 August, 2006; indebted to Melita Cristaldi for this information.

8. See David Bacon (2008) *Illegal People. How Globalization creates Migration and Criminalizes Immigrants*, Boston, Massachusetts: Beacon Press.

9. Shaykh 'Abd al Wahid Pallavicini (1998) 'Identita` e Differenze' (Identity and Differences), paper presented at the international conference, "Il Mare che Unisce. Scuola, Europa e Mediterraneo' (The Sea that Unites. School, Europe and the Mediterranean), Sestri Levante, Italy, 22-24 October, 1998.

10. Ahmed Moatassime (2000),'Mediterraneo fra plurilinguismo e pluriculturalita`' (The Mediterranean. Between Linguistic pluralism and Cultural Pluralism) in Giovanni Pampanini (ed) *Un Mare di Opportunita`. Cultura e Educazione nel Mediterraneo del lll Millenio* (A Sea of Opportunity. Culture and Education in the Mediterranean in the lll Millenium), Rome, Armando Editore, p. 113.

11. Carlos Alberto Torres (1998) op.cit p. 254.

12. Ministero della Pubblica Istruzione (1998), Mappa dei progetti italiani sul Mediterraneo' (Maps of Italian projects in the Mediterranean), Commissione Nazionale sull' Educazione Interculturale (National Commission forIntercultural Education) , Ministero della Pubblica Istruzione (Ministry of Education), p. 6.

13. Wright, H. K. (2009) Handel Kashope Wright talks to the project about Interculturalism vs Multiculturalism, Youth in

Canada, USA and Europe, his relationship with project founder, Joe Kincheloe and critical pedagogy's influence on his own work. Webcast, University of British Columbia, June 10, Montreal: The Paulo & Nita Freire International Project for Critical Pedagogy, McGill University.

14. Peter McLaren, (1997), *Revolutionary Multiculturalism: Pedagogies of Dissent for the New Millenium*, Boulder, Co., Westview Press, p. 230.

15. Antonia Darder (2011) *A Dissident Voice*, New York: Peter Lang; Antonia Darder (2011) *Culture and Power in the Classroom* (20th anniversary edition), Boulder, Colorado: Paradigm.

16. Peter Mayo (2005) ' Adult Education in the Mediterranean' and Shahrzad Mojab (2005) 'Adult Education in the Middle East' in Leona English (Ed.), *The International Encyclopedia of Adult Education* New York and Basingstoke: Palgrave-Macmillan; See also GRALE Report, Confintea V1, Hamburg: Unesco.

17. John Daniel (2005) *Education for All in the Arab World*, Unesco, 25th January http://www.portal.unesco.org/edu cation/en/ev, p. 6 Quoted by Hassan R. Hammoud (2006), Adult Illiteracy in the Arab World' in *Adult Education and Development*, No. 66 http://www.iiz-dvv.de/index.php?art icle_id=208&clang=1

18. See Antonia Darder's interview with Carmel Borg and myself in *A Dissident Voice* and in Carmel Borg and Peter Mayo (2007), *Public Intellectuals, Radical Democracy and Social Movements. A Book of Interviews*, New York and Frankfurt: Peter Lang.

19. Ngugi Wa Thiong'O (1986), *Decolonising the Mind. The Politics of Language in African Literature*, Portsmouth: Heinemann; London: James Currey; Nairobi: EAEP.

20. Henry A Giroux (1992) *Border Crossings Cultural Workers and the Politics of Education*, New York, Routledge.

21 George. J. Sefa Dei (1997), *Anti-Racism Education. Theory and Practice*, Halifax, Fernwood Publishing, pp.81, 82. Dei refers to hooks' work: bell hooks (1994), *Feminist Theory. From Margin to Centre*, Boston, South End Press.

22 See Nawal El Saadawi (1997) op. cit, Magda Adly in Borg and Mayo (2007) op cit., See the Associazione Donne del Mediterraneo's website: http://www.donnedelmediterraneo.org/intro.php Accessed on 10th December 2006.

23. Istituto Regionale di Ricerca Sperimentazione e Aggiornamento Educativi - Regional Institute for Educational Research, Experimentation and Update.

24. Mahmoud Elsheikh (1999), 'Le omissioni della cultural italiana' (the omissions of Italian culture) in *L'Islam nella Scuola* (Islam in schools), Innocenzo Siggillino (ed.), Editore Franco Angeli, pp. 30-45. p. 47.

25. See Edoardo Galeano (2009). *Open Veins of Latin America.* London: Serpent's Tail.

26. Frantz Fanon (1963), *The Wretched of the Earth*, New York, Grove Press Inc., p. 296. For a discussion on the issue of Scientism and racism, see Paulo Freire and Donaldo Macedo (2000), 'Scientism as a form of racism' in Stan Steiner, Mark Krank, Peter McLaren and Robert Bahruth (eds.), *Freirean Pedagogy, Praxis and Possibilities. Projects for the New Millenium*, New York: Falmer Press.

27. Mahmoud Salem Elsheikh, op.cit., p. 38. See also Gramsci with respect to Palencia in Notebook (Quaderno 16) (note 5) in Antonio Gramsci (1975), *Quaderni del Carcere* (Valentino Gerratana Ed.), Turin: Einaudi, as underlined by Derek Boothman (2007) 'L'Islam negli articoli giornalistici gramsciani e nei 'Quaderni del Carcere' 'in *NAE. Trimestrale di Cultura*, Vol. 18, pp. 65-66 –argument in pages 65-66. See also Tim Wallace-Murphy (2006), *What Islam did for Us. Understanding Islam's Contribution to Western Civilization*, London: Watkins Publishing.

28. Lê Thánh Khôi (1999), *Educazione e Civilta` Le società di ieri* (Education and Civilisation. Yesterday's Societies) (Giovanni Pampanini trans.), Rome, Armando Editore, p. 444; Lê Thánh Khôi (2000), 'Il Mediterraneo e il Dialogo fra le Civilta` '(The Mediterranean and Dialogue among Civilisations) in Giovanni Pampanini (ed.), *Un Mare di Opportunita`. Cultura e Educazione nel Mediterraneo del lll Millenio* (A Sea of Opportunity. Culture and Education in the Mediterranean in the lll Millenium), Rome, Armando Editore, p. 58.

29. Literal translation from Italian in Mahmoud Elsheikh (1999), op.cit. p.38.

Chapter 9

1. Previously appeared as a review of Linda Herrera and Asef Bayat (eds.) (2010), *Being Young and Muslim. New Cultural Politics in the Global South and North*, Oxford University Press in *Policy Futures in Education*, 10(1), 128-134. http://dx.doi.org/10.2304/pfie.2012.10.1.128

2. Linda Herrera and Asef Bayat (eds.) (2010) *Being Young and Muslim. New Cultural Politics in the Global South and North*, New York and Oxford: Oxford University Press.

3. Henry Giroux (2001), *Public Spaces/Private Lives. Beyond the Culture of Cynicism*, Lanham: Rowman & Littlefield.

Chapter 10

1. Previously published as Herrera, L and Mayo, P (2012), 'The Arab Spring, Digital Youth and the Challenge of Work' in *Holy Land Studies*, Vol. 11, No.1 (May). Permission to republish granted by Edinburgh University Press.

2. See http://www.guardian.co.uk/commentisfree/2011/jan/29 /egypt-mubarak-tunisia-palestine.

3. See interview 'A frozen revolution?', Dr Abd El Aziz Hegazy interviewed by Bertrand Borg in *The Times* (Malta), 15

November,2011, http://www.timesofmalta.com/articles/view /20111115/local/A-frosen-revolution-.393960. Accessed 16 November 2011.

4. See Linda Herrera. 'Egypt's Revolution 2.0: The Facebook Factor' in *Jadaliyya*. February 12, 2011. http://www. jadaliyya.com/pages/index/612/egypts-revolution-2.0_the-facebook-factor

5. See the many contributions to the book discussed in the previous chapter: Linda Herrera and Asef Bayat (eds.) (2010), *Being young and Muslim. New Cultural Politics in the Global South and North*, New York and Oxford: Oxford University Press.

7. Electronic exchange with Tahrir Square protestor carried out 8 July 2011.

8. See footnote 17 in Peter Mayo (2007), 'Gramsci, The Southern Question and the Mediterranean' in *Mediterranean Journal of Educational Studies*, Vol. 1, No. 2, pp. 1-17. http:// www.um.edu.mt/__data/assets/pdf_file/0004/39379/24_MJES _1222007.pdf Reproduced from an interview with Dall'Olio by Michael Grech in his book, *Knisja tat-Triq* (Street Church), Malta, 2006.

9. Electronic exchange with Tahrir Square protestor carried out 8 July 2011.

10. Noam Chomsky (2011) *September 11. Was there an alternative? (updated and expanded after the assassination of Osama Bin Laden, with a new introduction)*, New York: Open Media book.

Chapter 11

1. I am indebted to Professor M. Kazim Bacchus for his suggestions concerning an earlier version of the article and Vincent Caruana for his suggestions concerning certain sections of the same piece.

2. CHOGM –Commonwealth Heads of Government Meeting.

3. See his interview with Roger Dale and Susan Robertson in

Globalisation, Societies and Education, 2, 2, 2004.

Chapter 12

1. Peter McLaren (1994) *Life in schools. An introduction to critical pedagogy in the foundations of education.* New York & London: Longman.
2. Peter D Thomas (2011) in *The Gramscian Moment. Philosophy, Hegemony and Marxism,* Chicago, IL: Haymarket Books.
3. See Gramsci's notebook xxii on Americanism and Fordism in *Quaderni del Carcere* (Valentino Gerratana ed.), 1975, 4 Volumes, Turin: Einaudi.
4. See Thomas, op. cit, pp. 200-201.
5. Lavoie, M. and Roy, R, (1998) *Employment in the knowledge-based economy: A growth accounting exercise for Canada,* Ottawa: Applied Research Branch, Human Resources Development Canada, in David W. Livingstone, (2004) The Learning Society: Past, present and future views (R.W. B. Jackson Lecture, 2004). OISE/University of Toronto, October 14. Available at www.wallnetwork.ca (website of the Research Network on the Changing Nature of Work and Lifelong Learning –WALL, OISE/UT).
6. Phil Brown, Hugh Lauder and David Ashton (2010). *The Global Auction. The Broken Promises of Education, Jobs and Incomes,* New York: Oxford University Press.
7. See Leona English and Peter Mayo (2012), *Learning with Adults. A Critical Pedagogical Introduction,* Rotterdam and Taipei: Sense publishers.
8. See, for example, Bill Williamson (1998), *Lifeworlds and Learning. Essays in the theory, philosophy and practice of Lifelong Learning,* Leicester: NIACE; Kenneth Wain (2004), *The Learning Society in a Postmodern World. The Education Crisis,* New York and Frankfurt: Peter Lang.
9. The following section is a revised version of an entry on *'Education and political thought'* in the Encyclopedia of

Modern Political Thought, CQ Press (Sage).

See Henry Giroux (2005) *Schooling and the Struggle for Public Life: Critical Pedagogy in the Modern Age* (second updated edition), Boulder: Paradigm.

10. Michael Apple (1993) *Official Knowledge. Democratic Education in a Conservative Age*, New York & London: Routledge.

11. Antonia Darder, (2001) *Dissident Voice*, New York: Peter Lang.

12. Paula Allman (2010) *Critical Education Against Global Capitalism. Karl Marx and Revolutionary Critical Education*, Rotterdam & Taipei: Sense Publishers.

13. Sara Delamont (2003) *Feminist Sociology* London: Sage.

14. Angela Miles (1996), A, *Integrative Feminisms: Building Global Visions*, New York and London: Routledge.

15. Mary Belenky, Blythe Clinchy, Nancy Goldberger, and Jill Tarule, (1986). *Women's ways of knowing: The development of self, voice and mind.* New York. Basic Books.

16. Joe Kincheloe (1993), *Critical Pedagogy Primer*, New York: Peter Lang, 1993.

17. George Sefa Dei, (1998) *Anti-racism education: Theory and practice*, Halifax NS: Fernwood.

18. Ngugi Wa Thiong'o (1986) *Decolonizing the Mind. The Politics of Language in African Literature.* Oxford: James Currey & Heinemann, p.16.

19. Mike Oliver (1990), *The Politics of Disablement*, London & New York: Macmillan.

20. Edmund O'Sullivan, (1999) *Transformative Learning. Educational Vision for the 21st Century*, London: Zed Books.

21. Raymond Williams (1989) *Resources of Hope. Culture, Democracy and Socialism,* (Robin Gable ed.) London and New York: Verso.

About the Author

Peter Mayo is Professor in the Department of Education Studies, Faculty of Education, University of Malta. He is also a member of the 'Collegio docenti' for the research doctoral programme in Educational Sciences and Continuing Education at the Università degli Studi di Verona. He teaches/researches in sociology of education and adult education. His authored books include *Gramsci, Freire and Adult Education* (Zed Books, 1999) which has subsequently been published in six other languages, *Liberating Praxis* (Praeger, 2004; Sense, 2009) which won an AESA Critics Choice award, *Learning and Social Difference* (with C. Borg, Paradigm, 2006), *Learning with Adults. A Critical Pedagogical Introduction* (with L. English, Sense, 2012) and the forthcoming *Echoes from Freire for a Critically Engaged Pedagogy* (Continuum, 2012). Last year he won the best comparative and international research paper in Higher Education award granted by the Higher Education SIG of the Comparative International Education Society.

zero
books

Contemporary culture has eliminated both the concept of the
public and the figure of the intellectual. Former public spaces –
both physical and cultural – are now either derelict or colonized
by advertising. A cretinous anti-intellectualism presides,
cheerled by expensively educated hacks in the pay of
multinational corporations who reassure their bored readers
that there is no need to rouse themselves from their interpassive
stupor. The informal censorship internalized and propagated by
the cultural workers of late capitalism generates a banal
conformity that the propaganda chiefs of Stalinism could only
ever have dreamt of imposing. Zer0 Books knows that another
kind of discourse – intellectual without being academic, popular
without being populist – is not only possible: it is already
flourishing, in the regions beyond the striplit malls of so-called
mass media and the neurotically bureaucratic halls of the
academy. Zer0 is committed to the idea of publishing as a
making public of the intellectual. It is convinced that in
the unthinking, blandly consensual culture in which we live,
critical and engaged theoretical reflection is more important
than ever before.